MW01251335

HEAR, O HEAR MY PRAYER, O LORD:

Classic Hymns of Worship and Praise
&
Songs in the Taizé Style

VOL. I

Charles C. Cooke

PRESS

PREFACE

Singing is one of the most expressive and fulfilling ways of worshipping God. It gives people unity of spirit and voice in their offer of praise and thanksgiving. It vocalizes the prayers of many. I count myself among this group.

From an early age, the great Christian hymns of the church have always had a powerful impact on me; many of which were committed to memory not only from the Sunday church services but also from the morning assembly at the elementary and secondary schools I attended. Once exposed to these wonderful hymn tunes, one never forgets and they become a constant companion throughout one's Christian journey.

Each new generation makes its own contribution to the repertoire of songs of praise to Almighty God and this one is no different with its offering of hymns, worship songs and choruses.
This hymnal is my attempt to add to the richness of those stately hymns from my youth which still resonate with me and evoke passion-filled praise.

My hope is that your faith is strengthened, as mine has been, as you sing these hymns and you are drawn closer to God. May this hymnal be an additional tool in your personal, church and ministry life as you do His work!

I thank God for His perfect gift of music and for inspiring me on this project.

ACKNOWLEDGEMENTS

This hymnal would not have been possible without the incredible help, dedication, commitment and mentorship of Jason D. Locke who transformed my melodic and harmonic offerings in such a way that they became worthy of being shared with others. His great musicianship, rich and profound knowledge of hymnody is truly a blessing. It was a delight to work with him on this project.

I thank my beloved wife, June, who was unwavering in her support throughout this process. Our Christian journey together is strengthened daily through God's love.

I thank my siblings, Richard, Lucille, (late Norma), Wilfred, Mavis and Denise for their love and support as they contributed to my exposure to the church from early childhood.

I thank Arthur E. Smith and Veleyne A. Amsterdam for their contributions to this hymnal. Their texts have been truly inspirational and a blessing and extended the challenge of creativity. I thank my many friends, especially Marge, who were encouraging and supportive during what seemed like unproductive periods and setbacks.

This hymnal is dedicated to the memory of my mother, Mildred Gwenyth Cooke, whose singing and humming of those great hymn tunes of the church as she carried out her daily chores surely seeded the love of music in her son.

Dear Grace:

Thank you for your supportive and influential nature in the community.

May these hymns resonate with you in a special way drawing you ever closer to Almighty God.

With love and best wishes,

Charles C. Corke

August 27, 2014

¹ Sing to the LORD a new song;
sing to the LORD, all the earth.

² Sing to the LORD, praise his name;
proclaim his salvation day after day.

Psalm 96

How Awesome Is The Lord Most High!

1

How awesome is the Lord Most High, the great King over all the earth! Psalm 47:2

Charles C. Cooke

Moderato ♩ = 108

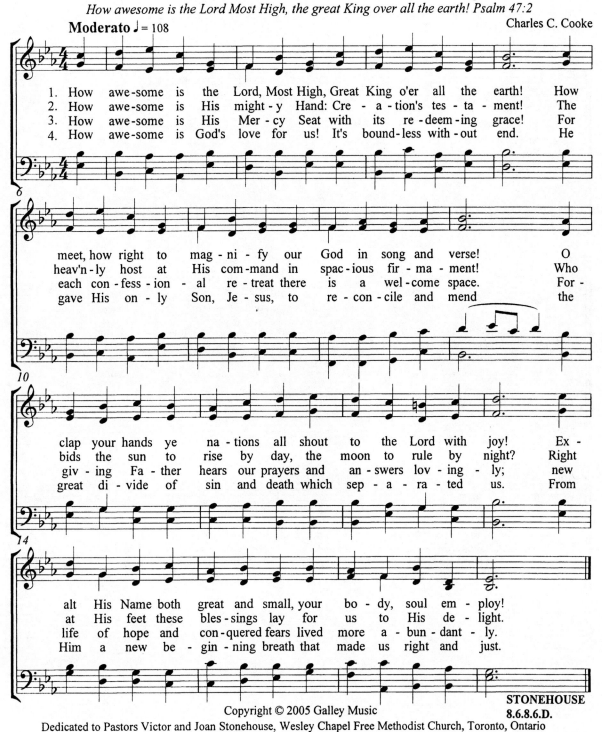

1. How awe-some is the Lord, Most High, Great King o'er all the earth! How
2. How awe-some is His might-y Hand: Cre - a-tion's tes - ta - ment! The
3. How awe-some is His Mer - cy Seat with its re-deem-ing grace! For
4. How awe-some is God's love for us! It's bound-less with-out end. He

meet, how right to mag - ni - fy our God in song and verse! O
heav'n-ly host at His com-mand in spac-ious fir - ma - ment! Who
each con-fess-ion - al re-treat there is a wel-come space. For -
gave His on - ly Son, Je - sus, to re-con-cile and mend the

clap your hands ye na - tions all shout to the Lord with joy! Ex -
bids the sun to rise by day, the moon to rule by night? Right
giv - ing Fa - ther hears our prayers and an - swers lov - ing - ly; new
great di - vide of sin and death which sep - a - ra - ted us. From

alt His Name both great and small, your bo - dy, soul em - ploy!
at His feet these bles - sings lay for us to His de - light.
life of hope and con-quered fears lived more a - bun - dant - ly.
Him a new be - gin - ning breath that made us right and just.

Copyright © 2005 Galley Music

STONEHOUSE
8.6.8.6.D.

Dedicated to Pastors Victor and Joan Stonehouse, Wesley Chapel Free Methodist Church, Toronto, Ontario

2
Sing Praises to the Lord!

Praise the Lord. Sing to the Lord a new song... Psalm 149:1b

Charles C. Cooke

Jason D. Locke

Moderato ♩ = 100

1. Sing prais-es to the Lord! Sing prais-es to the King! Who
2. Sing prais-es to the Lord, O, ev-'ry breath-ing thing! Let
3. Sing prais-es to the Lord! For His sal-va-tion comes to
4. Sing prais-es to the Lord! Let psalm-o-dy roll on! With-

1. re-con-ciled the world to Him; has done a new thing! Give
2. cym-bals clash and trum-pet sound! Let an - thems ring! The
3. ev-'ry hum-ble, con-trite heart that ov - er - comes the
4. in His pres-ence joy a-bounds to heights be - yond. Let

1. glo-ry to His Name in heav'n and earth a - dored! The
2. Lord, God takes de - light in those with rev-'rent fear who
3. snares of sin to live in His com-mand-ing light. It
4. cease-less hours of praise be our re-sound-ing core! We

JASON
6.6.8.5.6.6.8.6.

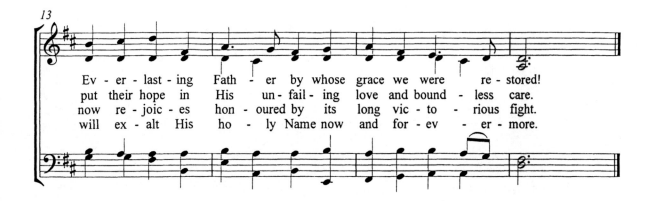

Ev - er - last - ing Fath - er by whose grace we were re - stored!
put their hope in His un - fail - ing love and bound - less care.
now re - joic - es hon - oured by its long vic - to - rious fight.
will ex - alt His ho - ly Name now and for - ev - er - more.

Lord, Your Word Lives On

3

Heaven and earth will pass away, but My words will never pass away. Matt.24:35

Moderato ♩ = 80

Charles C. Cooke

1. Lord, Your Word lives on and on; Truth to guide for ev - 'ry one.
2. On Your Word the faith - ful feed nour - ished like the plant - ed seed
3. All the sto - ries of great faith show us how to live to - day.
4. Lord, the lead - ers that You sent: out of E - gypt Mo - ses went.
5. Je - sus Christ, The Liv - ing Word, came to save a bro - ken world.

Though the earth will pass a - way, it will stand and e'er hold sway.
wel - com - ing the fall - ing rain, bring - ing forth ful - fill - ing grain.
A - bram trust - ed and o - beyed. Noah pre - pared whilst un - dis - mayed.
Da - vid was a might - y king; psalms of praise to You he'd sing.
Praise and pow'r and maj - es - ty, Lord, are Yours e - ter - nal - ly.

Copyright © 2007 Galley Music

BREWMAY
7.7.7.7.

4 From Nothing You Created Heaven and Earth

In the beginning, God created the heavens and the earth. Gen. 1:1

Moderato ♩ = 100

Charles C. Cooke

1. From noth-ing You cre - a - ted hea - ven and earth. E -
2. You deemed the light to be the day, dark - ness the night; the
3. And ev -'ry liv - ing crea - ture per - fect - ly made. Ac -

merg - ing from the dark - ness the un - i - verse gave birth. Al -
sun and moon in splen - dor pro - vid - ing ve - ry light. Al -
cord - ing to its own kind each one was thus ar - rayed. Al -

might - y God, the Fa - ther, where noth - ing - ness pre - vailed, You
might - y God, the Fa - ther, You gave the earth its food. Pro -
might - y God, the Fa - ther, in Your own like - ness then, You

reached a - cross the void with love. Won - drous works dis - played.
nounc - ing Your de - light, You saw, it was "ve - ry good".
breathed sus - tain - ing life to man in E - den's gar - den.

STEPHENSON
12.13.13.13.

Dedicated to Rev. Dr. John Stephenson, St. Timothy's Agincourt Anglican Church, Toronto, Ontario

The Heavens Display Your Glory, Lord

5

The heavens declare the glory of God; Psalm 19:1a

Arthur E. Smith

Charles C. Cooke

Moderato ♩ = 90

1. The heav'ns de-clare Your glo-ry, Lord, while earth re-sounds with praise. And day by day their voice is heard, they tell of God's great ways. In ev-'ry speech and lan-guage known through-out the un-i-verse, Your wis-dom is most clear-ly shown to peo-ples so di-verse.

2. O Lord, You gave such per-fect laws to touch, con-vert the soul. En-list me in Your right-eous cause to make the wound-ed whole! Your prom-ise makes my heart re-joice. Your stat-utes are most pure. Your judge-ments true, Your ten-der voice for-ev-er shall en-dure.

3. Your Word is sweet-er, yea, by far than hon-ey from the comb. Your pre-cepts shine bright as a star that guides the lost back home. Lord, keep my soul from will-ful sin, con-trol the things I do! Lord, make me pure with-out, with-in thus I will live for You.

ROSANNA
8.6.8.6.D.

Lord, God Almighty
(God of the Universe, Creator Most High)

...who made the great lights...the sun to govern the day...
the moon and stars to govern the night... Psalm 136:7-9

Veleyne Amsterdam

Charles C. Cooke

Moderato ♩ = 100

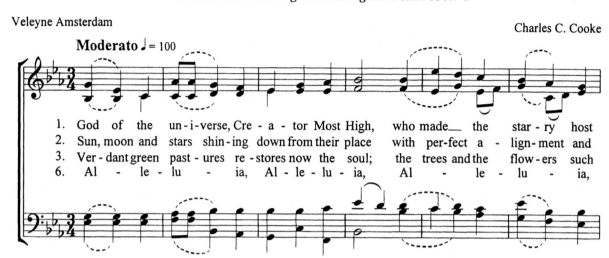

1. God of the un-i-verse, Cre - a - tor Most High, who made the star - ry host
2. Sun, moon and stars shin-ing down from their place with per-fect a - lign-ment and
3. Ver - dant green past - ures re -stores now the soul; the trees and the flow-ers such
6. Al - le - lu - ia, Al - le-lu - ia, Al - le - lu - ia,

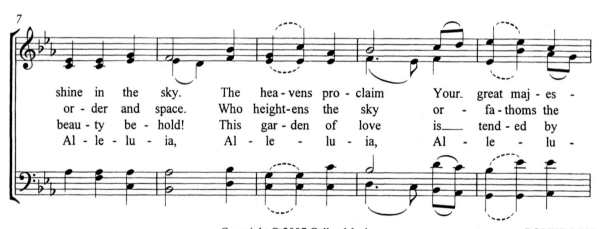

shine in the sky. The hea - vens pro - claim Your great maj - es -
or - der and space. Who height-ens the sky or - fa - thoms the
beau - ty be - hold! This gar - den of love is tend - ed by
Al - le - lu - ia, Al - le - lu - ia, Al - le - lu -

POMEROON
11.11.10.13

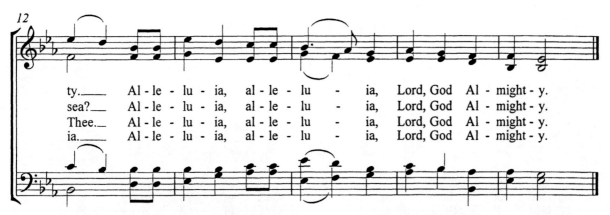

ty.___ Al - le - lu - ia, al - le - lu - ia, Lord, God Al - might - y.
sea?___ Al - le - lu - ia, al - le - lu - ia, Lord, God Al - might - y.
Thee.___ Al - le - lu - ia, al - le - lu - ia, Lord, God Al - might - y.
ia.___ Al - le - lu - ia, al - le - lu - ia, Lord, God Al - might - y.

4. Seasons will change and unerringly bring
The snowflakes of winter and blossoms of spring.
Great, glorious King all praise be to Thee.
Alleluia, alleluia, Lord, God Almighty.

5. Glories of summer: sun blazes the sky;
The falling of leaves show autumn is nigh.
These blessings, behold, are given by Thee.
Alleluia, alleluia, Lord, God Almighty.

The Earth Is Filled With Your Love

7

Charles C. Cooke

Text: Psalm 119:64

Moderato ♩ = 70

The earth is filled with Your love, O___ Lord. Teach me,___

teach me Your de - crees, O Lord. The Your de - crees, O Lord.

8

God of All Glory

They will speak of the glorious splendor of your majesty. Psalm 145:5

Veleyne Amsterdam

Charles C. Cooke

Moderato ♩ = 104

1. God of all glo - ry, God of all might,
God of all wis - dom, God of all light: we
praise and a - dore you in hea - ven so bright. O

2. God of all strength and God of all pow'r,
God of cre - a - tion. hill, dale and flow'r: Your
Name be ex - al - ted each mo - ment and hour! O

3. God of all bless - ings, God of all peace,
God of the vic - t'ry, God of the feast: most
won - der - ful Sa - viour Your love ne - ver cease. O

4. God of all heights, and God of all depths,
God of all car - ing, God who has wept: we
thank You for prom - is - es faith - ful - ly kept. O

5. God of all maj - es - ty, God of all grace,
God of all beau - ty God of all race: Your
pre - sence trans - cend - ing all time and all space. O

VELEYNE
Irregular Meter

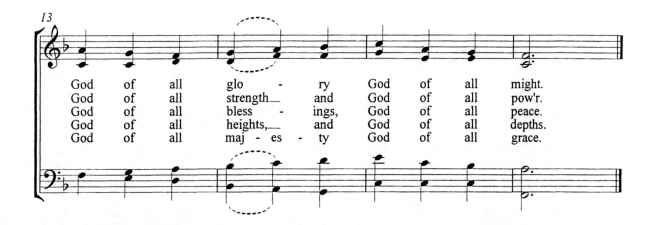

God of all glo - ry God of all might.
God of all strength and God of all pow'r.
God of all bless - ings, God of all peace.
God of all heights, and God of all depths.
God of all maj - es - ty God of all grace.

In Your Presence Joy Abounds

9

... You will fill me with joy in Your presence... Psalm 16:11

Charles C. Cooke

Moderato ♩ = 86

1. In Your pres - ence, joy a - bounds to heights of pleas - ant pla - ces.
2. On - ly now my heart has known the path of life with glad - ness.
3. Let re - joic - ing seize the soul and lift the flames of pas - sion
4. Lord, to You, all prais - es be re - sound-ing with thanks - giv - ing

You have made my lot se - cure with ov - er - flow - ing gra - ces.
For to dwell a - part from You are dark - some nights of sad - ness.
and re - lease the glow of love in sweet com - pel - ling fash - ion!
from the saints in glo - ry now and those a - mong the liv - ing.

FULLER
7.7.7.7.

10 The Sunrise Shows Your Faithfulness, O Lord

...the Maker of heaven and earth, the Lord... remains faithful forever. Psalm 146:6

Moderato ♩ = 90

Charles C. Cooke

1. The sun-rise shows Your faith-ful-ness to us, O Lord, each day. You
2. The morn-ing dew that nes-tles on the stem of ev-'ry flow'r; the
3. The la-bour that a-waits our hands or-dained by hea-ven's breath. For

watched us o'er the dark-some night and held us in Your sway. The
'wake-ning song-bird's tune-ful cry an-nounce Your awe-some pow'r. The
Je-sus Christ, Him-self, has toiled with care in Naz-a-reth. So

light that wash-es o'er the earth for ev-'ry eye to see, pro-
gen-tle rain-drops from the sky is na-ture's sooth-ing balm, as
may we learn from Him each day our du-ty to ful-fill and

claims the realm of Je-sus Christ for all e-ter-ni-ty.
ten-der mer-cies flow from Your Most Gra-cious, Might-y Hand.
rest as-sured at ev-en-tide we sought to do Your will.

INDUSTRY
8.6.8.6.D.

Lord, I Desire to Worship You

11

Exalt the Lord our God and worship at His footstool... Psalm 99:8 (TEV)

Arthur E. Smith

Charles C. Cooke

Moderato ♩ = 94

1. Lord, I de - sire to wor - ship You in Spir - it and in Truth. Let
2. So grant it Lord, that my whole heart, my bo - dy soul and mind cease
3. My pleas - ures Lord, be found in Thee not seek - ing earth - ly fame for
4. O, let me nev - er be con - tent to see poor sin - ners die! Help
5. Draw souls to Christ a - bun - dant - ly to has - ten His re - turn! For

all I think and say and do be this my one pur - suit.
sin - ful ways. Make this new start in Christ my pleas - ures find!
all a - round me I can see such fol - lies bring - ing shame.
me to lead them to re - pent and on Your grace re - ly.
such I wait, though pa - tient - ly, my heart for this doth yearn.

Copyright © 2009 Galley Music

OLD MANOR
C.M.

Create in Me a Clean Heart, O Lord

12

Text: Psalm 51:10 (NKJV)

Charles C. Cooke

Moderato ♩ = 64

Cre - ate in me a clean heart, O God. O__ God.

Copyright © 2010 Galley Music

13   What Joy Your People Feel Today!

All things are full of labour... Ecc. 1:8a (NKJV)

Charles C. Cooke

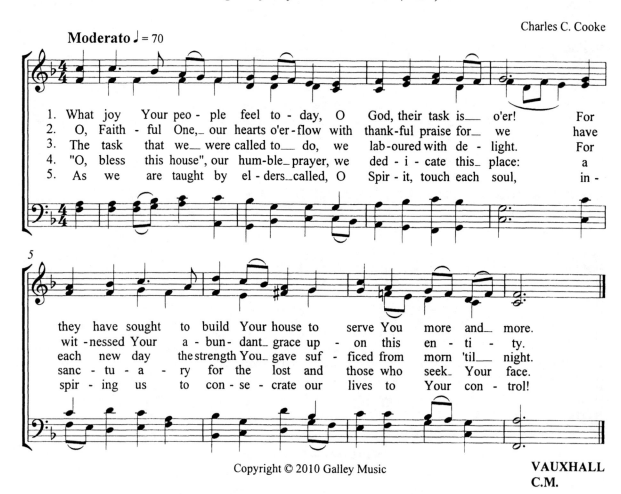

Moderato ♩ = 70

1. What joy Your peo - ple feel to - day, O God, their task is____ o'er! For
2. O, Faith - ful One,__ our hearts o'er - flow with thank-ful praise for__ we have
3. The task that we__ were called to__ do, we lab-oured with de - light. For
4. "O, bless this house", our hum-ble__ prayer, we ded - i - cate this__ place: a
5. As we are taught by el - ders__called, O Spir - it, touch each soul, in -

they have sought to build Your house to serve You more and__ more.
wit -nessed Your a - bun- dant__ grace up - on this en - ti - ty.
each new day the strength You__ gave suf - ficed from morn 'til__ night.
sanc - tu - a - ry for the lost and those who seek_ Your face.
spir - ing us to con - se - crate our lives to Your con - trol!

VAUXHALL
C.M.

6. Let every breath resound with praise
   O come, rejoice and sing!
   In fellowship, we worship You
   Our One, Eternal King.

7. All honour, glory be to God
   The Father we adore.
   All glory be to Christ, the Son
   And Spirit evermore!

Dedicated to Vauxhall Methodist Church, Christ Church, Barbados

Lo, A Night of Praise Beginning

I will lie down and sleep in peace, for you alone, O LORD,
make me dwell in safety. Psalm 4:8

14

Charles C. Cooke

Moderato ♩ = 88
Descant last stanza

6. Glo-ry be to Thee, O Fath-er. Glo-ry be to Thee, O Son.

1. Lo, a night of praise be-gin-ning with a song of love to Thee,
2. As the hues of twi-light sig-nal through the sun's re-treat-ing glare
3. Guid-ed through our toil-some jour-ney now the day is at an end
4. When the arms of sleep em-brace us to the dream-filled world we're lost,

Glo-ry be to Thee, O Spir-it while all end-less a-ges run.

thank-ful for a day spent win-ning one more soul for min-is-try.
we will trust the Lord, Most Faith-ful, ev-er rest-ing in His care.
grant us peace in quiet as-sem-bly as our wea-ry bod-ies mend.
ev-en there may we see Je-sus lov-ing-ly up-on the cross.

Copyright © 2007 Galley Music

KINGSLAND
8.7.8.7.

5. Lord, in Thee we dwell in safety
And in Thee find sweet repose.
May your gracious love and mercy
Cover us when eyes shall close.

6. Glory be to Thee, O Father;
Glory be to Thee, O Son;
Glory be to Thee, O Spirit
While all endless ages run.

15 Commit to the Lord and Give Him Your Plans

Commit to the Lord whatever you do and your plans will succeed. Prov. 16:3

Charles C. Cooke

Moderato ♩ = 90

Descant last stanza

5. Be - fore you em - bark on the works you hold dear, com -

1. Com - mit to the Lord and give Him your plans. What -
2. The Lord will find fav - our and grant you suc - cess; the
3. The toil of the hands or the cre - a - tive mind when
4. Ob - serve His com - mands and His stat - utes each day! On
5. Be - fore you em - bark on the works you hold dear sub -

mit to the Lord in hum - ble prayer. He

ev - er you do is all by His Hands. Your
One slow to ire and swift to bless. Each
of - fered to Him suc - cess you will find. He
them med - i - tate, dis - cern - ing His way! "Be
mit to the Lord in hum - ble prayer. He

LOCKE
11.10.11.11.

16   Lord, God In You I Trust

In You, O Lord, I have taken refuge... Psalm 71:1a

Moderato ♩ = 90

Descant last stanza

Charles C. Cooke

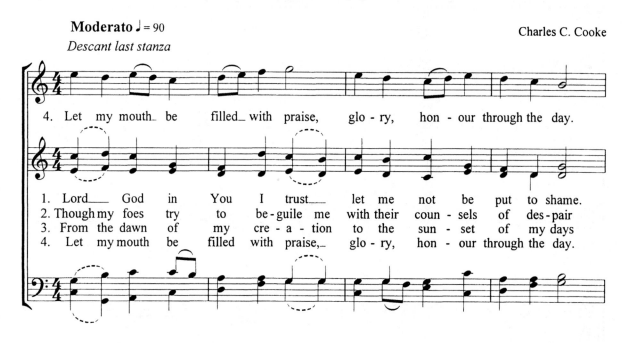

4. Let my mouth be filled with praise, glory, hon - our through the day.

1. Lord___ God in You I trust___ let me not be put to shame.
2. Though my foes try to be - guile me with their coun - sels of des - pair
3. From the dawn of my cre - a - tion to the sun - set of my days
4. Let my mouth be filled with praise,___ glory,___ hon - our through the day.

My___ De - fend - er, my___ De - liv - 'rer. keep me___ in___ Your per - fect sway!

You are my a - bid - ing for - tress lead me in Your path, the same.
You, O Lord, are al - ways with me guard - ing 'gainst the tempt - er's lair.
You, O Lord, have kept me safe - ly, fixed se - cure - ly in___ Your gaze.
My De - fend - er, my De - liv - 'rer. keep me in Your per - fect sway!

LUCILLE LENORA
8.7.8.7.

To Live Is to Grow

Grace and peace be yours in abundance through the
knowledge of God and of Jesus our Lord. 2 Pet. 1:2

Charles C. Cooke

1. To live is to grow in the grace of the Sav-iour, a
2. Re - mem - ber what you have re - ceived from Him dai - ly, that

Friend from our birth, un - fath-om - ly so! Each day is a grac-ious ful -
which you must keep. O, keep and re - pent! Each gift is a per-fect and

fill - ment of prom-ise, a - bound-ing in love, the faith-ful ones know.
boun - ti - ful bless-ing from God's grac-ious Hand so lav-ish - ly spent.

IRVIN
12.10.12.10.

18 How Happy Are the Faithful!

A happy heart makes the face cheerful. Proverbs 15:13

Charles C. Cooke

Moderato ♩ = 100

1. How hap-py are___ the faith-ful whose souls have been re-deemed! They
2. To those who fol-low Je-sus re-joice when called to share the
3. Re-joic-ing in___ the Sav-iour, en-rich-ment to the soul like
4. The fa-ces of___ the faith-ful re-veal their in-most joy with
5. All glo-ry to___ the Fath-er whose won-drous Name we praise. All

trust-ed and___ are grate-ful to join those saints___ es-teemed. The
news of His___ sal-va-tion, His ten-der___ love___ and care. For
in-cense sweet to sa-vour, like pre-cious bur-nished gold. For
read-i-ness___ for ser-vice their ta-lents___ to___ em-ploy give
glo-ry to___ Lord Je-sus who for all___ things were made. All

hea-vens raise their an-thems in wel-com-ing the best. The
they know in their be-ing the tur-moil they have felt when
ev-'ry non-be-liev-er who does not know the Lord can
what they have been giv-en with un-re-serv-ed love. Their
glo-ry to the Spir-it who fills each con-trite heart! O

GALL HILL
7.6.7.6.D.

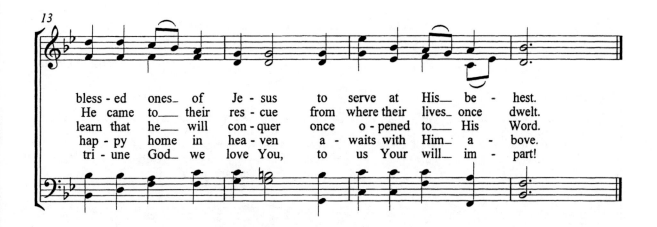

bless - ed ones_ of Je - sus to serve at His_ be - hest.
He came to_ their res - cue from where their lives_ once dwelt.
learn that he_ will con - quer once o - pened to_ His Word.
hap - py home in hea - ven a - waits with Him_ a - bove.
tri - une God_ we love You, to us Your will_ im - part!

The Joy of the Lord

19

... Do not grieve, for the joy of the Lord is your strength. Neh. 8:10b

Charles C. Cooke

Andante ♩ = 70

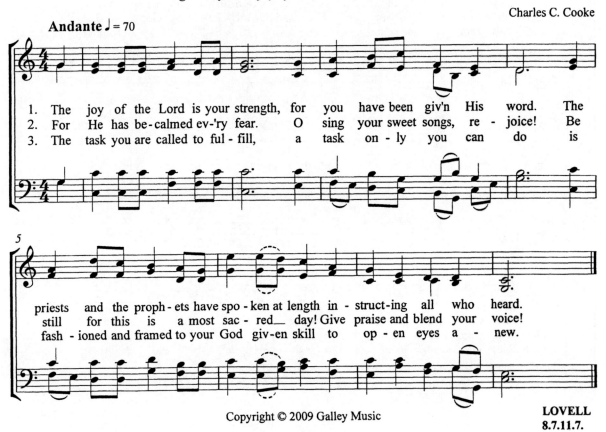

1. The joy of the Lord is your strength, for you have been giv'n His word. The
2. For He has be - calmed ev - 'ry fear. O sing your sweet songs, re - joice! Be
3. The task you are called to ful - fill, a task on - ly you can do is

priests and the proph - ets have spo - ken at length in - struct - ing all who heard.
still for this is a most sac - red_ day! Give praise and blend your voice!
fash - ioned and framed to your God giv - en skill to op - en eyes a - new.

LOVELL
8.7.11.7.

20   O Faithful, Bring Your Praises

Is anyone happy? Let him sing songs of praise. James 5:13b

Charles C. Cooke

Moderato ♩ = 100

1. O faith-ful, bring your prais - es and sing your songs to Him. As
2. For - ev - er through the a - ges the faith of saints re - vealed their
3. O sing re-dempt-ion an - thems with reed and strings in tune. Let

ones who are com - mend - ed as right-eous and whose sin is
one de - sire for ser - vice and fol - low - ing God's lead. The
cym - bals keep re - sound - ing and fil - ling ev - 'ry room! The

nev - er - more re - mem - bered, the prom - ise God has giv'n. O
cer - tain - ty of ho - ping for what they could not see brought
Lord in heav'n is lis - t'ning and find - ing great de - light in

look to - wards that ci - ty which Christ pre - pared in heav'n!
blest re - wards in - vok - ing His great a - bun - dan - cy.
each blest child who loves Him with heart and soul and might.

STEPHEN MOORE
7.6.7.6.D.

Praise Awaits You, O God, in Zion

21

Praise awaits You, O God, in Zion... to you all men will come. Psalm 65: 1-2

Text: Psalm 65: 1 - 2

Charles C. Cooke

Moderato ♩ = 100

Praise a - waits You, O God, in Zi - on. To you our vows will be, will be ful - filled. O, You who hear prayer, to You all men will come. Praise a - waits You, O God, in Zi - on.

THERESA
Irregular meter

22   O, The Righteous Are Glad

...the righteous are glad and rejoice in His presence;
they are happy and shout for joy. Psalm 68:3 (TEV)

Charles C. Cooke

Moderato ♩ = 80

1. O, the right-eous are glad and re-joice in His pre-sence. O, the
2. O, the right-eous will serve with their gift-ed re-sour-ces to pro-
3. O, the right-eous will pray. They will pray with-out ceas-ing and with
4. O, the right-eous are known for their love of the Sav-iour. O, the
5. O, the right-eous de-sire on-ly one af-fir-ma-tion: "Faith-ful

right-eous are glad and de-light in His Name. They give
claim the Good News of the king-dom of Christ. His com-
love in-ter-cede for all peo-ple in need. Un-be-
right-eous are known for their trust in the Lord. They de-
ser-vant, well done!" from their Mas-ter and King. Then in

hon-our and thanks to God on their jour-ney each day. They are
mand-ment of love and care for our bro-ther they keep. Nev-er
knownst, they are lift-ed up to the throne of God's grace with as-
sire but to live for Him with com-mun-ion in-crease; ev-er
glo-ry with won-drous love, a-do-ra-tion and praise, they will

ISOLINE COOKE
Irregular Meter

hap - py and shout for joy prais - ing Him all the way.
seek - ing of world - ly praise, His ap - prov - al they reap.
sur - ance of an - swered prayer that the right - eous em - brace.
seek - ing to do His will with ex - pect - an - cy, peace.
wor - ship Al - might - y God end - less - ly through the age.

Taste and See

23

Text: Psalm 34:8

Charles C. Cooke

Maestoso ♩ = 80

Taste and see that the Lord is good.

Taste and see that the Lord is good.

24 Our Tongue With Joyful Shouting

... our toungues with songs of joy. Then it was said among the nations,
"the Lord has done great things fo them." Psalm 126:2

Charles C. Cooke

Moderato ♩ = 100

1. Our tongue with joy - ful shout - ing for what the Lord has done will
2. All na - tions now con - fess - ing the treas - ure they have found; re -

touch the man - y doubt - ing what they could e'er be - come: a
count - ing ev - 'ry bless - ing with faith se - cure and sound. Be -

part of His great ar - my trans - formed by love and grace; re -
yond all trib - u - la - tion they see the gold - en shore where

ceiv - ing ten - der mer - cy a - vail - ing ev - 'ry race.
Christ's per - fect o - bla - tion is theirs for - ev - er more.

GOLDEN RIDGE
7.6.7.6.D.

By His Grace

...it is by grace you have been saved. Eph. 2:5b

Charles C. Cooke

1. By His grace we are spared ev-er-last-ing strife. All our sins washed a-way we claim new life. For our faith we're re-moved to our home on high when our Lord shall ap-pear in the twink-ling of an eye.

2. From His hand we are blessed most a-bun-dant-ly. Gifts of love flow and yet we do not see. Ope' our eyes, pre-cious Lord, so that thank-ful praise be our hearts' one de-sire ev'-ry mo-ment of our days.

3. With His peace we find rest for the troub-led mind. World-ly cares, doubts and fears are left be-hind. So in prayer we lift up Christ in joy-ful song for our sole rest-ing place: on His bos-om we be-long.

MARYSTOWN
11.10.10.13.

26 The Grace That Keeps My Soul at Peace

And we... are being transformed into His likeness with ever-increasing glory. 2 Cor. 3:18

Moderato ♩ = 116

Charles C. Cooke

1. The grace that keeps my soul at peace with liv-ing streams of bold de-sire to
2. The mer-cy God be-stows on me when-e'er I fall His love I see. When

claim the way of God's High Priest with driv-en faith, con-sum-ing fire. A
fears be-set most cer-tain-ly His com-fort stills, my heart is free. O,

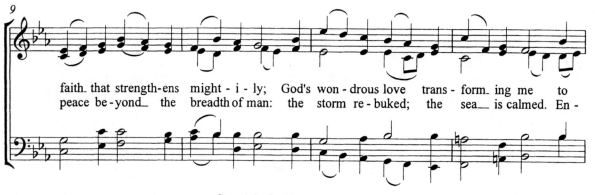

faith that strength-ens might-i-ly; God's won-drous love trans-form-ing me to
peace be-yond the breadth of man: the storm re-buked; the sea is calmed. En-

CHERRY DRIVE
8.8.8.8.D.

be____ like His_ be - lov - ed Son._ God's plan_ for each   and ev - 'ry one.
joined to share the news to all__ may I,___ with faith, ac - cept_ the call.

Keep Thy Servant Close Forever

The Lord watches over you... will keep you from all harm.
He will watch over your life. Psalm 121: 5a, 7

27

Charles C. Cooke

Moderato ♩ = 90
Descant last stanza

3. All whose hope_ is in Christ_ Je - sus know Thy ser -vant's fate:

1. Keep Thy   ser - vant close   for - ev - er   al -ways in Thy   care,
2. O,   the   touch of   love re - flect - ed   in such ten - der eyes
3. All whose hope   is   in   Christ Je - sus   know Thy ser -vant's fate:

one__ of peace, e - ter - nal_ glo - ry   in their now_ trans - fig -ured   state.

'twas but for a fleet -ing   mo -ment paced their pil - grim jour -ney here.
bring - ing joys of time -less beau - ty through their im - age in the skies.
one   of peace, e - ter - nal glo - ry   in their now trans - fig -ured state.

HAYLEI PILGRIM
8.5.8.7.

28 Rend Our Hands From Worldly Treasure

"Do not store up for yourselves treasures on earth...". Matt. 6:19a

Charles C. Cooke

Moderato ♩ = 72

1. Rend our hands from world-ly treas-ure, Lord, let us yield it all to___ Thee!
2. What is there to prize the fleet-ing? Vain the pur-suit of tear-ful dross!
3. Cleanse our bod-ies from all crav-ing that brings us harm and will des-troy!
4. Blest are they who look to hea-ven where on-ly last-ing treas-ures___ stand!

Thou hast giv'n be-yond all meas-ure Thy pre-cious life to set us free.
When our hearts are in Thy keep-ing all we have earned must count as loss.
Spir-it come in ways a-maz-ing, mak-ing us ho-ly filled with joy!
Ser-ving Christ, the Sav-iour, Ri-sen, bound for the bless-ed prom-ised land!

Loose the___ bonds of our pos-ses-sions! Each temp-ta-tion nul-li-fy!
Kin-dle___ now our flame to fol-low Thee, O Lord, with fer-vent ways.
Now re-leased in mind and bod-y from the dark-ness in-to light,
Let our___ needs be Christ-in-spir-ing, thirst-ing for the Liv-ing God!

FELL AVENUE
8.8.8.8.8.7.8.7.

So Thy al - tar of con - fes - sions is not sul - lied, Lord, Most High.
May we meet the new to - mor - row claim - ing Christ with end - less praise.
Christ, to Thee, all hon - our, glo - ry, Thou hast giv - en us new sight.
He, a - lone our souls de - sir - ing as we walk this earth - ly sod!

Those Who Cling to Worthless Idols 29

Those who cling to worthless idols forfeir the grace that could be theirs. Jonah 2:8

Charles C. Cooke

Text: Jonah 2:8
Psalm 31:16, 19

Moderato ♩ = 68

1. Those who cling to worth - less i - dols for - feit the grace that could be theirs. But
2. Let Your face shine on your ser - vant save me in Your un - fail - ing love. How

I, with a song of thanks - giv - ing, will sac - ri - fice__ to You.
great is Your good - ness and mer - cy which You be - stowed on me!

SAUNDERS
8.8.9.6.

30

Flesh Won't Glory in His Presence

No flesh should glory in His presence. 1 Cor. 1:29 (NKJV)

Charles C. Cooke

Moderato ♩ = 90

1. Flesh won't glo - ry in His pres-ence nor re-fract the light from Him.
2. O, the im - age on our can - vas that the world should clear - ly see

For we are in our ex - ist - ence soiled in un - re - pen - tant sin.
should be on - ly that of Je - sus, Lord in great - est maj - es - ty.

Let no i - dle boast o'er - take us claim - ing works and good - ly deeds!
Cast a - side our blind am - bit - ion for the spot - light's pierc - ing rays!

Christ a - lone should be our fo - cus, full sub - mis - sion as He__ leads!
Choose to live for His great mis - sion ev - 'ry mo - ment of our__ days!

Copyright © 2009 Galley Music

ASHTON HALL
8.7.8.7.D.

God Is So Good to Us

Good and upright is the Lord... Psalm 25:8a

31

Charles C. Cooke

1. God is so good to us, more than we de - serve.
2. God is so good to us. Look up - on the cross!
3. God is so good to us. Love be - yond de - gree!

He is most mar - vel - ous, Him a - lone we serve.
There, see Lord Je - sus sav - ing us the lost.
Ho - ly and right - eous there at Cal - va - ry.

E'en though we fall from grace through our own mis - step,
Would we but hon - our Him with a change-filled heart.
Lord, may we lift our voice in thanks-giv - ing praise.

we find a rest - ing place one the Lord has kept.
o - pened to let Him in where He'll ne'er de - part?
Bless us as we re - joice all our pil - grim days.

PINELANDS
6.5.6.5.D.

32 Come To Him!

Believe on the Lord Jesus, and you will be saved. Acts 16:31

Moderato ♩ = 80

Charles C. Cooke

1. Come to Him! He sets you free. Come a - vail this mys - ter - y.
2. Come to Him! Cast fears a - side. He knows all what - e'er be - tide.
3. Come to Him you lost and 'lone! In His arms you find your home.
4. Come to Him and choose the way! Trust in Him and watch and pray!

Know His grace is yours to claim. Read His Word and call His name.
Dark - ness is con - sumed by light. Christ, The One, He shines so bright.
Lift - ed by His awe - some pow'r, help is yours this ve - ry hour.
Right - eous - ness will fill your soul. Bro - ken ves - sels are made whole.

Come to Him! The chains of sin are re - leased by on - ly Him.
Come to Him who calmed the sea, tri - umphed ov - er Cal - va - ry.
"Come to Him", the sim - ple plea; one that leads to vic - to - ry.
Come to Him with thank - ful praise! Wor - thy is the Lamb who saves.

ST. DAVID'S
7.7.7.7.7.7.

A Vessel Prepared

But we have this treasure in jars of clay to show that this
all-surpassing power is from God and not from us. 2 Cor. 4:7

Moderato ♩ = 96

Charles C. Cooke

1. A ves-sel pre-pared to wor-ship the King! Made clean by His grace, my
2. What He has cre-a-ted, so He has sealed. His mark on my face thus

trib-ute to bring! Most use-ful and sanc-ti-fied now for His
now is re-vealed. The Pot-ter of pot-ters has formed me to

work! In Him, I be-lieve, through Him, I as-sert.
be a ves-sel that serves by His own de-cree.

CONNELL TOWN
11.10.11.10.

34 O, That We Might Humble Be

Humble yourselves before the Lord, and He will lift you up. James 4:10

Charles C. Cooke

Moderato ♩ = 70
Descant, last stanza

4. Ho-ly Je-sus, Ser-vant, Friend, washed the feet of mor - tals.

1. O, that we might hum-ble be, nev-er seek-ing glo - ry!
2. Vain di-ver-sions prom-ise pow'r with al-lur-ing gran - deur
3. "Hearts of ser-vice", it must be our re-frain most sure - ly;
4. Ho-ly Je-sus, Ser-vant, Friend, washed the feet of mor - tals.

What a less-on to be learned ex-it-ing these por - tals!

Self-less, un-as-sum-ing hearts should re-flect our sto - ry!
on - ly bring-ing dark des-pair when they start to fal - ter.
for those lift-ed up on high are the meek and low - ly.
What a less-on to be learned ex-it-ing these por - tals!

CARRINGTON
7.6.7.6.

Hear, O Hear My Prayer, O Lord

Hear my prayer, O LORD; listen to my cry for mercy. Psalm 86:6

Charles C. Cooke

Moderato ♩ = 90

1. Hear, O hear my prayer, O Lord. Hear my hum-ble cry.
2. When I fall on bend-ed knee at the al-tar call.
3. Ho-ly, ho-ly, ho-ly Lord; this my rev-'rent plea:

Hear, O hear my prayer O Lord. Do not
When I fall on bend-ed knee, I sur-
Ho-ly, ho-ly, ho-ly Lord make me

pass me by. Do not pass me by.
ren-der all. I sur-ren-der all.
more like Thee. make me more like Thee.

DENISE ERNESTA
7.5.7.5.

36 His House of Prayer

These I will bring to My holy mountain and give them joy in My house of Prayer. Isaiah 56:7

Andante ♩ = 70

Charles C. Cooke

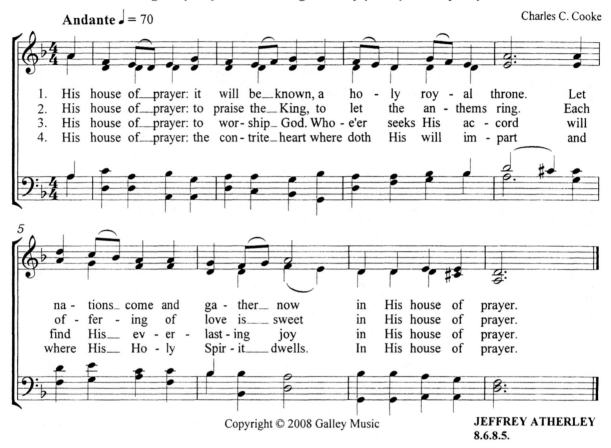

1. His house of__prayer: it will be__known, a ho-ly roy-al throne. Let
2. His house of__prayer: to praise the__King, to let the an-thems ring. Each
3. His house of__prayer: to wor-ship__God. Who-e'er seeks His ac-cord will
4. His house of__prayer: the con-trite__heart where doth His will im-part and

na-tions__come and ga-ther__now in His house of prayer.
of-fer-ing of love is__sweet in His house of prayer.
find His__ev-er-last-ing joy in His house of prayer.
where His__Ho-ly Spir-it__dwells. In His house of prayer.

JEFFREY ATHERLEY
8.6.8.5.

37 Restore Us to Yourself, O Lord

Text: Lam. 5:21

Charles C. Cooke

Moderato ♩ = 70

1.2.3... | Finale

Re-store us to Your-self, O Lord that we may re-turn. Re-turn.

O Guide Me

...guide me in Your truth and teach me. Psalm 25:5

Charles C. Cooke

1. O guide me pre - cious Lord_____ to fol - low where you
   (prec - ious Lord)
2. O teach me how to pray_____ re - fresh my thoughts a -
   (how to pray)
3. O let_ Thy bless - ings flow_____ on this poor heart of
   (Bless- ings flow)

lead_____ that I_ might_ live to pro - claim Your
(Where You lead)
new_____ so words ex - pressed each and ev - 'ry
(thoughts a - new)
mine_____ as I_ re - flect in the af - ter
(heart of mine)

word and to do Your_ ev - 'ry deed._____
day re - main pure with_ love for You._____
glow I will know all_ gifts are Thine._____

ELKHORN
6.6.8.8.

38

39 Quietness and Peace Consume

Be still and know that I am God. Psalm 46:10

Charles C. Cooke

Moderato ♩ = 82

1. Qui - et - ness and peace con - sume the hall - ways of the heart that's
2. Sol - i - tude will let us hear His voice of calm to bring a
3. "Rest a while", the Sav - iour said, His call to be re - stored. En -
4. May each thought breathe out His Name with re - ver - en - tial awe! The

giv - en to the Lamb of God com - plete - ly, not in part. The
nec - es - sa - ry word that thrills the soul and make it sing. For
ter the realm of Christ, The King, in ma - jes - ty a - dored! The
near - er we draw un - to Him, to us near - er He'll draw. The

blank - ness of des - pair is wrought from ev - 'ry troub - led mind. De -
si - lence is not ours to fill when we seek full ac - cord. It
qui - et mo - ments lost in prayer bring strength un - to the soul. A
hu - man view we oft - en trust will al - ways lead a - stray and

DELSMAY-ELON
13.14.14.14.

liv - er - ance and hope once sought, the cap - tive now will__ find.
is e - nough to pause, be still, and know the Lord is__ God.
life en - vel - oped in His care for - ev - er is the__ goal.
cause His sweet re - pose and peace to flee from us to - day.

Come In Silence Before The Lord 40

If my people... will humble themselves and pray... then I will hear from heaven... 2 Chron. 7:14

Veleyne Amsterdam
Charles C. Cooke

Charles C. Cooke

Moderato ♩ = 76

1. Come in si - lence be - fore the Lord, se - cret - ly or in the pub - lic square.
2. Med - i - tate on His Word each day. Feed up - on its Truth with great de - sire.
3. Let the cloak of hu - mil - i - ty be the__ stand-ard that de - fines your state
4. Wait for His ev - er - guid - ing hand pa - tient - ly to do His sov-'reign will.
5. Wait in sil - ence to hear His voice. In the__ still - ness of each mo - ment then

Where, O where - ev - er you may be, praise the Lord in prayer.
Let your prayer for dis - cern - ment blaze as a ho - ly fire!
when ap - proach-ing His throne of grace in a prayer - ful wait.
He is faith - ful and will sup - ply means to then ful - fill.
o - pened hearts will re - ceive His Word with a loud "A - men".

ESSEQUIBO
8.9.8.5.

41 O Peace, Come Forth in Bounteous Light

May there be peace within your walls and security within your citadels. Psalm 122:7

Charles C. Cooke

1. O peace, come forth in boun-teous light and tow-er o'er the earth. And heal the na-tions to be-come a-new with heav'n-ly birth. The Lord's great tem-ple will be raised: a meet-ing place for all, to

2. May those who serve You be se-cure and peace be theirs with-in the ci-ta-del of qui-et rest. At last, Je-ru-sa-lem! The striv-ings of a-noth-er world are dis-tant and un-known. The

3. The call-ing of the Lord to heed His com-ing and pre-pare, is grace-filled in its cov-en-ant of won-drous love and care. The gath-'ring of His peo-ple blest, where thrones for judge-ment stand. The

ROSALIND JONES
C.M.D.

walk in His most ho - ly ways up - on His trum - pet call.
faith for that which was un - seen, they claim it as their own.
Prince of Peace will then de - clare those fav- oured by His   Hand.

O Blessed Jesus, Prince of Peace

For to us a child is born... And he will be called... Prince of Peace. Isaiah 9:6

42

Arthur E. Smith

Charles C. Cooke

Moderato ♩ = 80

1. O Bless-ed Je - sus, Prince of Peace, reign free - ly, Lord, in me; bid
2. O Bless-ed Je - sus, Prince of Peace, come now and spread good - will o'er
3. O Bless-ed Je - sus, Prince of Peace, as in the days of yore, in
4. O Bless-ed Je - sus, Prince of Peace, the world has suf - fered long. The
5. O Bless-ed Je - sus, Prince of Peace, sol - dier of peace I'll be. I'm

all my in - ner striv - ings cease that I might peace - ful be.
all the earth Your reign in - crease ex - ert Your sov -'reign will.
might and love Your strength re - lease 'til strife shall be no more.
might - y tram - ples right with ease, come Lord, cor - rect this wrong!
at Your ser - vice, Lord, do please e - quip, com - mis - sion me!

NELSON SPRING
C.M.

43 When God Has Touched Our Souls Anew

See I am doing a new thing! Isaiah 43:19a

Charles C. Cooke

Moderato ♩ = 90

1. When God has touched our souls a - new and framed our hearts like His, with
2. With teem-ing hope to fill each day to share with those we meet, we
3. O God of mer - cy, Faith-ful One, who sets the cap - tive free! When
4. A new thing, Lord, that You have done! Con-vict us to be - lieve that

un - sur-pass-ing grace we find em - bold-ened ways to live. The
ov - er-come what's in the way. Each vic - to - ry is sweet! The
our re - sourc - es are but gone for us You part the sea. And
when we dwell a - part from You we can-not then re - ceive the

pas - sions that we feared were lost for - ev - er in the maze of
nour - ish-ment that God pro - vides, the wis - dom He im - parts will
make a way for us to tread se - cure and safe and true but
liv - ing streams of good-ness borned from Your a - bun - dant ways. O

JENNIFER-M
8.6.8.6.D.

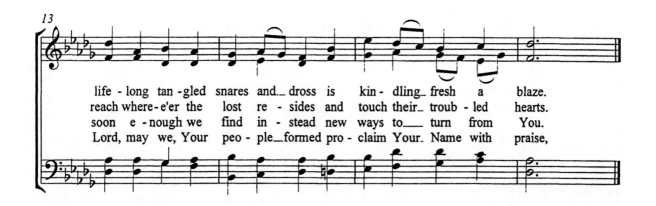

life - long tan -gled snares and dross is kin - dling fresh a blaze.
reach where- e'er the lost re - sides and touch their troub - led hearts.
soon e - nough we find in - stead new ways to turn from You.
Lord, may we, Your peo - ple formed pro - claim Your Name with praise,

A Searching God Looks Keenly On

We love because He first loved us. 1 John 4:19

Charles C. Cooke

Maestoso ♩ = 70

44

1. A search-ing God looks keen - ly on for that lost soul to come, to
2. Re - claim your joy, O prod - i - gal! A lov - ing Lord a - waits. Be

free - ly claim what's free - ly giv'n: His One A - noint - ed Son.
cov - ered with un - fath-omed grace on en - ter - ing His gates!

SARGEANT'S VILLAGE
C.M.

45 His Eyes Hath Never Left My Frame

The Lord watches over you... Psalm 121:5a

Moderato ♩ = 92

Charles C. Cooke

1. His eyes hath nev-er left my frame not ev-en for a mo-ment, e'en
2. He watch-es o'er the a-li-en, sus-tains the low-ly wid-ow. The
3. He nev-er slum-bers nor He sleeps. His eyes are on His peo-ple. And

though my sin had brought Him shame and suf-fer-ring and tor-ment. But
fa-ther-less find such a Friend a-mid the dark-est shad-ow. For
safe-ly on His bo-som keeps the lone-ly and the fear-ful. O

O, what love that flow-eth down from hea-ven and ab-solv-ing my
He is mer-ci-ful and just, pro-vid-ing for His child-ren. O
Lord, my God, O You a-lone will keep me e'er from fall-ing or

sin so I could wear a crown whilst I was still e-volv-ing.
won-drous grace, so mar-vel-lous! Let tongues re-peat this an-them.
cause my feet to strike a stone. You hear my ev-'ry call-ing.

PARKINSON FIELD
8.7.8.7.D.

Yearn Will We for Your Presence, Lord

46

As the deer pants for streams of water, so my soul pants for You, O God. Psalm 42:1

Charles C. Cooke

Moderato ♩ = 80

1. Yearn will we for Your pres-ence, Lord as deer pants for the wa - ter.
2. Day and night will our quest go on, rest - ing not for a mo - ment.
3. Yea, our hope rests up - on the Lord. All our praise will ex - tol___ Him.

Thirst - ing now for the liv - ing God each a son or a daugh - ter.
Learn - ing well what the saints have known suf - fer - ing ev - 'ry tor - ment.
When foes say "O, where is your God"? We can shout with thanks - giv - ing:

Our de - sire is to be re-stored by the One heav'n and earth a - dored.
Seek - ing You is our deep - est need. O, what joy when we all suc - ceed!
"Here's our Rock, and our Rest - ing Place! Our De - liv - 'rer who saves by grace!"

PIERCY WARD
8.7.8.7.8.8.

47 Seek The Lord and He Will Hear Us

I sought the Lord and He heard me. Psalm 34:4 (NKJV)

Charles C. Cooke

Moderato ♩ = 90

1. Seek the Lord and He_ will hear us, He a - waits our ev - 'ry call.
2. He has prom-ised us,_ His child-ren, faith - ful - ness, in - clin-ing ear

Reach-ing out to Christ, Lord Je - sus, brings sweet fel - low - ship to all.
to the cries that e'er_ so oft - en make for_ mo - ments of des - pair.

E - ven though the dark clouds ho - ver round a - bout our pil - grim way,
O, the cen - tre - piece of trust - ing is com -plete sur - rend -ered lives

He is our sus - tain - ing tow - er that our hearts find when we pray.
not when -e'er the storms are gust - ing but when stars_ are on the rise.

CHARLES RICHARD
8.7.8.7.D

Still Our Hope Is in The Lord

48

If only for this life we have hope in Christ... 1Cor. 15:19

Charles C. Cooke

Moderato ♩ = 90

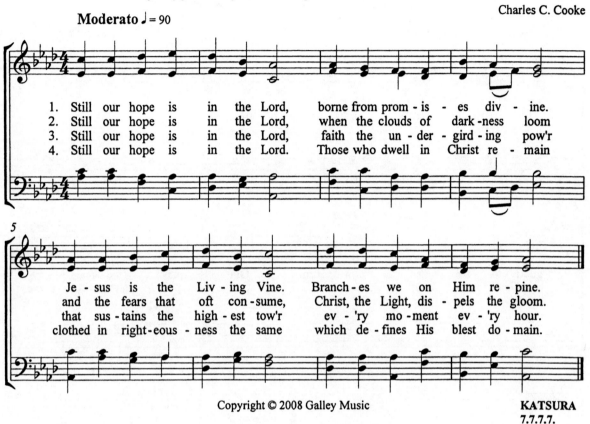

1. Still our hope is in the Lord, borne from prom - is - es div - ine.
2. Still our hope is in the Lord, when the clouds of dark -ness loom
3. Still our hope is in the Lord, faith the un - der - gird - ing pow'r
4. Still our hope is in the Lord. Those who dwell in Christ re - main

Je - sus is the Liv - ing Vine. Branch - es we on Him re - pine.
and the fears that oft con -sume, Christ, the Light, dis - pels the gloom.
that sus - tains the high - est tow'r ev - 'ry mo - ment ev - 'ry hour.
clothed in right-eous - ness the same which de - fines His blest do - main.

KATSURA
7.7.7.7.

5. Still our hope is in the Lord
   His commandments all to keep;
   Faithful Shepherd, may Your sheep
   Find repose when we shall sleep.

6. Still our hope is in the Lord.
   O what love to reassure!
   Unto Him our hearts adore
   Evermore and evermore.

49 God Is the Strength of My Long Aching Heart

... but God is the strength of my heart and my portion forever. Psalm 73:26b

Moderato ♩ = 80

Charles C. Cooke

1. God is the strength of my long ach-ing heart. O, it is good to be near Him. Oth-ers may find their de-light in the world, but He is my por-tion a - gain and a - gain.
2. Oft seen a - bun-dan-cy lures and de-ceives, caus-ing the sim - ple to stray._____ God will pro - nounce in the full - ness of time on those who de - cide they will go their own - way.

MILE-AND-A-QUARTER
10.8.10.11.

Strength In Waiting Is Our Goal

50

Wait on the Lord. Psalm 27:14a (NKJV)

Charles C. Cooke

1. Strength in wait - ing   is our goal.   He knows what the   fu - ture holds.
2. Be cour - a - geous   for the fight!   In the Lord we   take de - light.
3. Dwell with pa - tience   ev - 'ry day!   Claim His Word, its   gen - tle way!

Trust up - on the   Lord then brings   strength to   soar   on   eag - les' wings.
No - thing is   too   hard for Him.   Ev - 'ry   bat - tle   He will   win.
Truth re -vealed to   un - der -gird   each be - liev - er   who has   heard!

CAROLINE WEEKES
7.7.7.7.

In My Distress I Cried to the Lord

51

Text: Psalm 120: 1 (NKJV)

Jason D. Locke

Moderato ♩ = 70

In   my dis - tress   I   cried__ to the   Lord.

52 Walk In The Light

But if we walk in the light, as He is in the light,
we have fellowship with one another. 1 John 1:7a

Charles C. Cooke

Moderato ♩ = 50

1. Walk in the Light; live by the Truth com-port-ing to His like - ness! Claim
2. Christ is the Way, the Truth, the Life. Through Him we see God's king - dom. All
3. Find last-ing peace to rule your days be - yond all un-der - stand-ing! Cling
4. Lord, hide Your Word with - in our hearts lest we should sin a - gainst You! Pre-

fel-low-ship; know in your heart Christ's love and its for - give - ness! O,
oth-er ways be ban-ished dross! They on - ly bring des - truct-ion. As
to a grace so full and free, no debt is still out - stand-ing! En-
cepts to guide, stat - utes to keep, to med-i-tate and praise You. Bless-

to be made com - plete in Him! Grace that o'er-comes the
peo-ple of the Lord, be bold! Fol - low Him like the
ter His courts with songs of praise! Live with de - light! Walk
ed are they whose ways are pure! Help us, O Lord, to

COX ROAD
8.7.8.7.8.8.7.

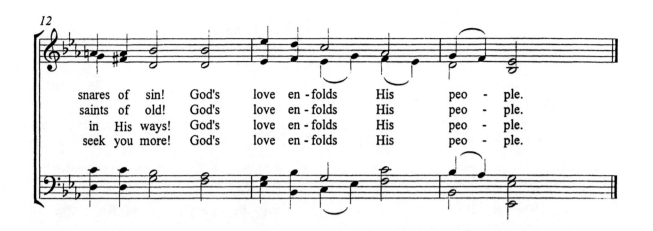

snares of sin! God's love en-folds His peo - ple.
saints of old! God's love en-folds His peo - ple.
in His ways! God's love en-folds His peo - ple.
seek you more! God's love en-folds His peo - ple.

The Fruit of Self-Control

53

... the fruit of the Spirit is ... self-control. Gal. 5:22

Charles C. Cooke

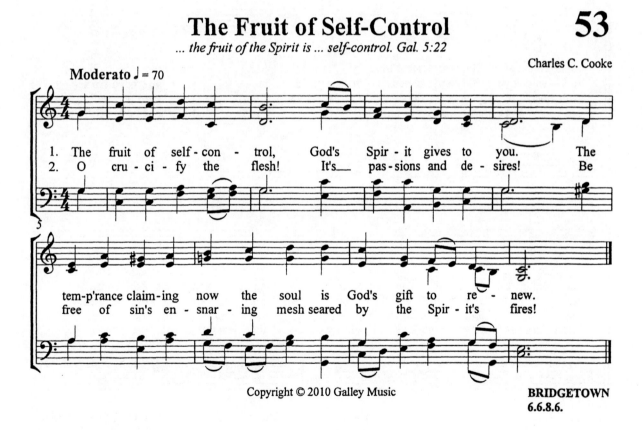

Moderato ♩ = 70

1. The fruit of self-con - trol, God's Spir-it gives to you. The
2. O cru - ci - fy the flesh! It's__ pas-sions and de - sires! Be

tem-p'rance claim-ing now the soul is God's gift to re - new.
free of sin's en - snar - ing mesh seared by the Spir-it's fires!

BRIDGETOWN
6.6.8.6.

54 The Way of Holiness

And a highway will be there; it will be called the Way of
Holiness. The unclean will not journey on it. Isaiah 35:8

Charles C. Cooke

Moderato ♩ = 80

1. The Way of Ho - li - ness, the high-way will be known that
2. The Way of Ho - li - ness, is safe and most se - cure for
3. The Way of Ho - li - ness, is joy-filled with de - light. This
4. The Way of Ho - li - ness, O en - ter through the gates! The

each child of God will_ most sure-ly tra-vel on. No-thing de-fil-ing,
all who love God and_whose con-trite heart is pure. They all have trust-ed,
path-way of splen-dor_shines thru' the dark-some night. God's Word a guid-ing
ci - ty of Zi-on_ in maj-es-ty a - waits. Bring songs of glad-ness,

no - thing un - clean will jour-ney or come near and has for - ev - er been.
they are re-deemed and are for-ev-er blest, join-ing the saints es-teemed.
lamp to the feet for all who fol-low Him, pro-claim a life com-plete.
bring songs of praise with love and faith-ful-ness that last through-out the age!

MAVIS FREDERICA
6.6.6.6.5.4.6.6.

Be Holy

But just as he who called you in holy, so be holy in all you do. I Peter 1:15

Charles C. Cooke

Moderato ♩ = 92

1. Be ho - ly. Be ho - ly as Christ___ is ho - ly. Be ho - ly. Be
2. Have mer - cy. Have mer - cy as God___ has mer - cy. Have mer - cy. Have
3. Be lo - ving. Be lov - ing as God___ is lov - ing. Be lov - ing. Be
4. Be gen - tle. Be gen - tle. The Ho - ly Ghost is gen - tle. Be gen - tle. Be

ho - ly as ho - ly as the Lamb. For as He who has call - ed you is
mer - cy for He has shown us how. He looked up - on our help - less state and
lov - ing for God Him - self is love. Re - turn to Him the love He shows each
gen - tle with His in - dwell - ing pow'r. His will is to trans - form the soul with

ho - ly Be ho - ly, most ho - ly. May all our com - port be.
sent His Son to die. Have mer - cy, more mer - cy. Fore - go an eye for eye.
mo - ment of the day. Be lov - ing, most lov - ing. Fol - low His path al - way.
pure hu - mi - li - ty. Be gen - tle, most gen - tle. Be filled with em - pa - thy.

NORMA GIFT
6.7.6.6.8.6.6.6.

56   Children of God

... now we are children of God, and what we will has not yet been made known. 1 John 3:2

Charles C. Cooke

Moderato ♩ = 85

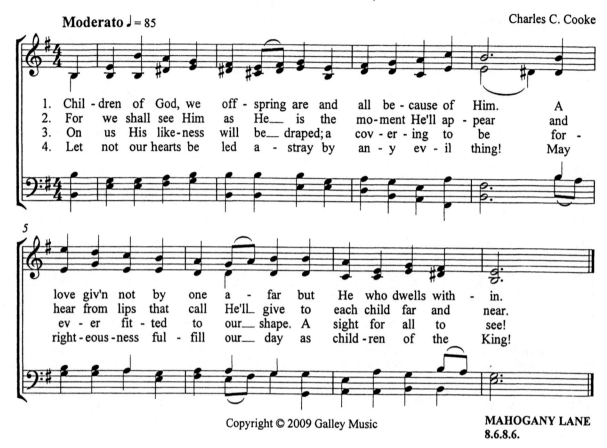

1. Chil-dren of God, we off-spring are and all be-cause of Him. A
2. For we shall see Him as He__ is the mo-ment He'll ap-pear and
3. On us His like-ness will be__ draped; a cov-er-ing to be for-
4. Let not our hearts be led a-stray by an-y ev-il thing! May

1. love giv'n not by one a-far but He who dwells with-in.
2. hear from lips that call He'll give to each child far and near.
3. ev-er fit-ted to our__ shape. A sight for all to see!
4. right-eous-ness ful-fill our__ day as chil-dren of the King!

MAHOGANY LANE
8.6.8.6.

5. No longer are we slaves again
   His Spirit we've received.
   Co-heirs with Him, we count as gain
   Because we have believed.

6. Children of God who shine like stars
   Throughout the universe!
   So pure and blameless, without scars
   Freed from sin's awful curse!

Virgin, You Have Found Great Favour 57

...Mary, you have found favour with God.
You will be with child and give birth to a son... Luke 1:30-31

Charles C. Cooke

Moderato ♩ = 80

5. Lord, like Ma - ry let us serve Thee with full bo - dy, mind and heart

1. Vir - gin, you have found great fav - our with Al - might-y God a - bove.
2. You've been blessed be - yond all meas - ure in your hum-ble state to find
3. Lo, the grace of your ac - cept - ance in the heart of one so young,
4. In re - joic - ing you have taught us that when God be - stows a task
5. Lord, like Ma - ry let us serve Thee with full bo - dy, mind and heart

to ful - fil and bring You glo - ry what Your sov - 'reign will im - part.

You will car - ry Christ, The Sav - iour, God in - car - nate full of love.
you've been giv - en heav - en's treas - ure to re - deem all hu - man kind.
see the glow up - on your coun - t'nance, hear the sweet re - ply you sung.
He will show - er bless - ings on us more than we could hope or ask.
to ful - fil and bring You glo - ry what Your sov - 'reign will im - part.

SOMERSALL
8.7.8.7.

58

In the Inn of Bethlehem

...she...placed him in a manger, because there was no room for them in the inn. Luke 2:7b

Charles C. Cooke

Moderato ♩ = 88

1. In the inn of Beth-le-hem O, there was no room for them. Not a
2. In the fields near Beth-le-hem shep-herds saw the an-gel then up-on
3. In the sky o'er Beth-le-hem shone the star the three wise men fol-lowed
4. From the heart of Beth-le-hem came sal-va-tion to all men. O, the

place to lay their head as they searched to find a bed but
hear-ing the good news left their lit-tle lambs and ewes and
from the O-ri-ent with most sin-gu-lar in-tent to
great, great love of God through His giv'n in-car-nate Word! The

God would o-pen up a way a-mid the bales of hay where
found the Sav-iour, Christ the Lord. With joy they spread the word and
find the bless-ed new born King and make their of-fer-ing. What
ba-by boy in man-ger stall would re-con-cile us all. Who-

FERN
7.7.7.7.8.6.6.6.

Je-sus would be born on that first Christ-mas morn.
wor-shipped God on high with praise to glo-ri-fy.
pre-sents to be-hold: in-cense and myrrh and gold!
e'er on him be-lieves, e-ter-nal life re-ceives.

From the Realms of Kingship Glory

59

Today in the town of David a Saviour has been born to you;
He is the Christ the Lord. Luke 2:11

Charles C. Cooke

Moderato ♩ = 80

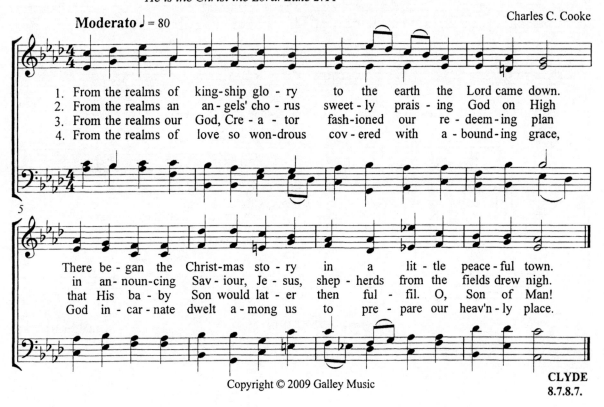

1. From the realms of king-ship glo-ry to the earth the Lord came down.
2. From the realms an an-gels' cho-rus sweet-ly prais-ing God on High
3. From the realms our God, Cre-a-tor fash-ioned our re-deem-ing plan
4. From the realms of love so won-drous cov-ered with a-bound-ing grace,

There be-gan the Christ-mas sto-ry in a lit-tle peace-ful town.
in an-noun-cing Sav-iour, Je-sus, shep-herds from the fields drew nigh.
that His ba-by Son would lat-er then ful-fil. O, Son of Man!
God in-car-nate dwelt a-mong us to pre-pare our heav'n-ly place.

CLYDE
8.7.8.7.

60 By Night, God's Glory Was Revealed

And there were shepherds living out in the fields nearby, keeping watch over their flocks at night. Luke 2:8

Descant: Last stanza
Moderato ♩ = 80

Charles C. Cooke

5. By night a choir of an-gels sang all prais-ing God on high: "Glo-

1. By night God's glo - ry was re - vealed be - fore the awe - filled eyes of
2. By night a - lone the wise men three from O - ri - ent a - far they
3. By night in lit - tle Beth - le - hem on low - ly sta - ble straw from
4. By night God's glo - ry took its form with tid - ings of great joy: to
5. By night a choir of an - gels sang all prais-ing God on high: "Glo-

ry to God!" their voi - ces rang through-out the star - lit sky,

shep - herds keep - ing watch a - field be - neath the o - pen skies.
jour - neyed on by proph - e - cy while guid - ed by a star.
shep - herds to the no - ble - men re - joiced at what they saw.
day the Sav - iour has been born a hum - ble ba - by boy.
ry to God!" their voi - ces rang through-out the star - lit sky,

GLORIA DANIEL
C.M.

O, Helper of the Fatherless

... You are the helper of the fatherless. Psalm 10:14b

Charles C. Cooke

Moderato ♩ = 80

1. O, Help - er of the fath - er - less, pro - tect Your peo - ple from all harm. Sur-
2. You hear, O Lord, th'af - flict - ed ones and lis - ten to their plain - tive cry. Your

round - ing us are foes of truth who feed up - on and cause a - larm. But
might - y Hand, the ref - uge sought, pro - tects from those who ter - ri - fy. De-

God who slum - bers not or sleeps will call the e - vil to ac - count. For
liv - er us from sword or snare and lead us to that place of peace! A

as he sows he al - so reaps in eq - ual kind and like a - mount.
place of rest be - yond com - pare where tongues of praise will nev - er cease.

JUNER
L.M.D.

62 Trusting, Trusting Little Children

From the lips of children and infants you have ordained praise... Psalm 8:2

Charles C. Cooke

♩ = 80

1. Trust - ing, trust - ing lit - tle child - ren. May our faith, like theirs, grow strong!
2. Sim - ple trust in hearts so ten - der, teach-ing mo - ments for the proud!
3. Prais - es mark their rad - iant be - ing, form the won - der in their eyes,
4. May we now re - write our sto - ry ech - o - ing the truths they know,

From their mouths the God of hea-ven is made known to old and young.
They ex - per - ience full sur - ren - der well be - fore they speak a - loud.
God's do - min - ion they are see - ing as they gaze the star - ry skies.
bring - ing God the great-est glo - ry, trust - ing Him for - ev - er - more.

LEAH
8.7.8.7.

63 Gifted From the God of Grace

Sons are a heritage from the LORD, children a reward from Him. Psalm 127:3

Charles C. Cooke

Moderato ♩ = 80

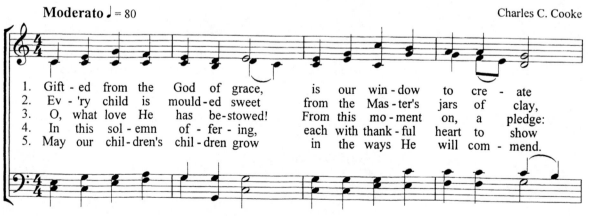

1. Gift - ed from the God of grace, is our win - dow to cre - ate
2. Ev - 'ry child is mould-ed sweet from the Mas - ter's jars of clay,
3. O, what love He has be-stowed! From this mo - ment on, a pledge:
4. In this sol - emn of - fer - ing, each with thank - ful heart to show
5. May our chil - dren's chil - dren grow in the ways He will com - mend.

ELLORA
7.7.7.7

through a glimpse of new-born life, now to Him we con - se - crate.
per - fect - ly with fin - est form bring-ing joy day aft - er day.
that His word we will e'er use 'gainst all e - vil as a hedge.
blessed by God's ful - fill - ing grace, we are His for - ev - er - more.
Let His bos - om be their rest faith - ful to the ve - ry end!

Come, Little Ones, Play at His Feet 64

"Let the little children come to me...". Luke 18:16

Charles C. Cooke

Moderato ♩ = 70

1. Come, lit - tle ones, play at His feet the feet of Je - sus are re - plete with
2. He calls the lit - tle ones to Him and warns us not to hin - der them: the
3. The joy of now these ear - ly years are sto -ried bless-ings when life's fears are
4. Cling to His gar -ments shin - ing bright to walk as child-ren of the light for
5. Cling to His hands with all your might those pier-ced hands that made it right to

love and care for you each day when as you grow and learn His way.
King-dom of our God be-longs to such as these, the ve - ry young.
cast up - on your wiz-ened face you will re - call this peace-ful place.
thus His King-dom you will be the mod - el of hu - mil - i - ty.
see the Fa - ther on His throne when comes the day you will go home.

LILLIAN
L.M.

65 "It is Written", Words to Ponder!

Jesus answered:"It is written, 'Man does not live on bread alone...'" Matt. 4:4

Moderato ♩ = 85

Charles C. Cooke

1. "It is writ - ten". Words to pon - der when temp - ta - tion brings its woes.
2. "It is I". All fear dis - pel - ling words when storm - y seas ap - pear.
3. "It is fin - ished". Words ful - fill - ing per - fect - ly God's Mas - ter Plan.

Wis - dom there to hold in won - der and to use a - gainst all foes.
Christ, His glo - rious pow'r com - pel - ling calm to reign for He is near.
On the cross the Sav - iour will - ing there to die for sins of man.

Pow - er rests with - in its pa - ges; might - y is the word of God!
O, the com - fort in that vis - ion of a Guid - ing Sav - iour, Friend!
Love, how won - drous in ex - press - ion in the sac - ri - fice He made!

Ev - er - last - ing through the a - ges; hope where - e'er the saints have trod.
Suc - cour to the souls in pri - son bro - ken spir - its He will mend.
An a - ton - ing gift from hea - ven for sin's debt is ful - ly paid!

BANNISTER
8.7.8.7.D.

The Dusty Roads He Walked

... news about Him spread through the whole countryside.
He taught in their synagogues... Luke 4:14b-15a

Charles C. Cooke

Moderato ♩ = 88

1. The dust-y roads He walked, all the day long. There fol-lowed as He talked an
2. In syn-a-gogues He taught. Schol-ars would draw. Most clev-er - ly they sought to
3. The sick, the lame He healed. De - mons took flight! With pow'r the blind re - vealed their
4. In par - a-bles He spoke. Spir - it-filled food! The fish and bread He broke to

ov - er-whelm-ing throng press - ing to hear the wis -dom He'd im -
trap Him with the Law. He knew their hearts and they would soon des -
joy with new-found sight. His gar - ments clutched in faith and deep be -
feed the mul - ti - tude! How God pro - vides! What bless-ings from His

part with words to cheer and fill the emp - ty heart.
pair for words like darts would pierce their lis - t'ning ear.
lief pre - sumed His touch which brought com-plete re - lief.
Hand! With love He guides to - ward the Prom-ised Land.

MAGNOLIA
6.4.6.6.4.6.4.6.

67 The Road to Jerusalem

As the time approached for Him to be taken up to heaven
Jesus resolutely set out for Jerusalem. Luke 9:51

Charles C. Cooke

Moderato ♩ = 76

1. The road to Je - ru - sa - lem was be - fore Him
2. He suf - fered up - on the cross where His bo - dy
3. The road to sal - va - tion runs right through Him.

fraught with the dan - ger of e - vil men. He re - so - lute - ly
bro - ken in tor - ment a - mid the dross showed what a lov - ing God
Take it and there - by be free from sin! Go to the wood - en cross

then set His face__ de - ter - mined to take__ our place.
would grace - ful - ly - en - dure all for to make__ us pure.
where Christ the Sav - iour died, go and be sanc - ti - fied!

THE ROAD TO JERUSALEM
Irregular Meter

Remain in Me

Text: John 15:4

Charles C. Cooke

Andante ♩ = 80

Re - main in___ Me and I will re - main in you. Re - main in___ Me and

I will re - main in you. No branch can bear fruit by it - self, it must re - main___

in___ the vine. It must re - main___ in___ the vine.___

ROCK DUNDO
Irregular Meter

69 Jesus Sealed the Master Plan

Then Jesus went with His disciples to a place called Gethsemane... Matt. 26:36

Charles C. Cooke

Moderato ♩ = 88

1. Je - sus sealed the mas - ter plan with His lone - ly walk
2. Je - sus bridged the great di - vide 'tween my fall - en soul
3. Je - sus Sav - iour, Lord and King: glo - ry to Thee now.

in the dark - est gar - den hour and His an - guished talk
and the Great Je - ho - vah, God. Through Him I am whole.
At Thy Name, both great and small, ev - 'ry knee shall bow.

with the Fa - ther. He would go with His cross to___ bear,
Love made mani - i - fest that day on a cross of___ shame,
Praise and hon - our be to Thee for Thy work com - plete.

pay - ing debts He did not owe, ones I could not pay.
nails and thorns en - dured for me, all to clear my name.
Keep me stead - fast 'til I'm home joy - ful at Thy feet.

WALTER
7.5.7.5.D.

Take This To Thy Comfort

70

"Take and eat, this is my body". Matt. 26:26b

Andante ♩ = 65

Charles C. Cooke

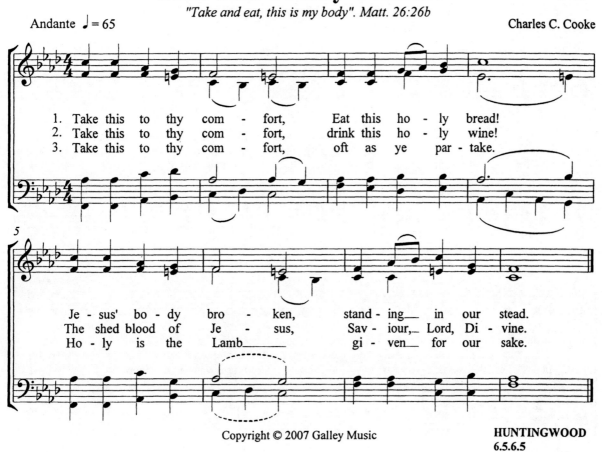

1. Take this to thy com - fort, Eat this ho - ly bread!
2. Take this to thy com - fort, drink this ho - ly wine!
3. Take this to thy com - fort, oft as ye par - take.

Je - sus' bo - dy bro - ken, stand - ing__ in our stead.
The shed blood of Je - sus, Sav - iour,__ Lord, Di - vine.
Ho - ly is the Lamb__ gi - ven__ for our sake.

HUNTINGWOOD
6.5.6.5

Born to Die

71

Charles C. Cooke

Moderato ♩ = 70

Born to die so I might live. A Bless - ed Sav - iour's life to give.

72 Hosanna! Crucify Him! Alleluia!
(The Shouts of Adulation in Welcome of the King)
"Hosanna to the Son of David". Matt 21:9

Moderato ♩ = 88

Charles C. Cooke

1. The shouts of ad - u - la - tion in welcome of the King to
2. The mul - ti - tude would soon dis - play their fic - kle hearts' de - sire and
3. Then in the ear - ly morn - ing the wo - men would ap - pear to

rule o'er all Je - ru - sa - lem and con - qu'ring ar - my bring. Ho -
seize up - on the Lamb of God with all - con - sum - ing ire. Cru - ci -
claim the Bless - ed Sav - iour, but lo, He was not there! Al - le -

san - na! Ho - san - na! The voi - ces raised to Thee. The
fy Him! Cru - ci - fy Him! They shout - ed to the sky. And
lu - ia! Al - le - lu - ia! With joy they un - der - stood that

KURUP
8.6.8.6.D.

prom - ised king has come and here He rides in ma - jes - ty!
nailed the Sav - iour to the cross and left Him there to die.
Christ had ris - en from the dead as He said He would.

On The Day That Has No Name

The next day, the one after Preparation Day... Matt. 27:62

73

Charles C. Cooke

Moderato ♩ = 88

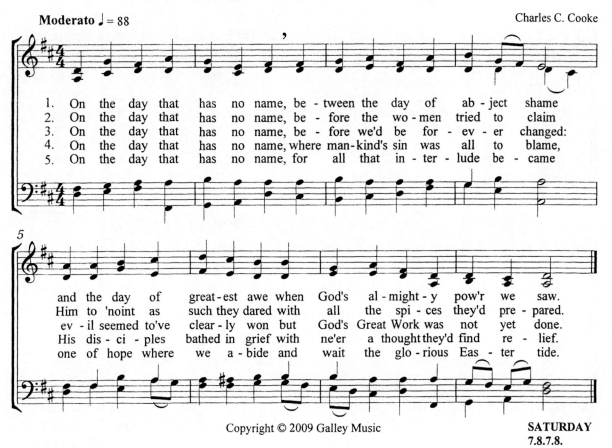

1. On the day that has no name, be - tween the day of ab - ject shame
2. On the day that has no name, be - fore the wo - men tried to claim
3. On the day that has no name, be - fore we'd be for - ev - er changed:
4. On the day that has no name, where man-kind's sin was all to blame,
5. On the day that has no name, for all that in - ter - lude be - came

and the day of great - est awe when God's al - might - y pow'r we saw.
Him to 'noint as such they dared with all the spi - ces they'd pre - pared.
ev - il seemed to've clear - ly won but God's Great Work was not yet done.
His dis - ci - ples bathed in grief with ne'er a thought they'd find re - lief.
one of hope where we a - bide and wait the glo - rious Eas - ter tide.

SATURDAY
7.8.7.8.

74

The One Eternal Sacrifice

... because by one sacrifice He Has made perfect
forever those who are being made holy. Heb. 10:14

Music by Charles C. Cooke
Text by Arthur E. Smith

Moderato ♩ = 90

1. The one___ e - ter - nal sac - ri - fice Christ of - fered
2. O, how___ could I such debt___ re - pay? What debt to
3. A liv - ing sac - ri - fice___ I'll give. My bo - dy
4. To this___ vile world I'll not___ con - form. I'll cast___ its
5. Come liv - ing Lord, have Your___ own way! Your al - tar

in my place.___ A par - don for sins it
Christ I owe!___ Dear Christ,___ my life, my
I pre - sent.___ I will___ serve Christ; for
ways be hind.___ Come Hol - ly Ghost, my
is my heart.___ Ac - cept___ my off - 'rings

did suf - fice, it saved me through God's good grace.___
truth, my way, O teach me Your heart to know!___
Him I'll live; for Him will my life be spent.___
heart trans - form, O come and re - new my mind!___
Lord, I pray, and nev - er from me de - part.___

NEVIS PEAK
8.6.9.7.

The Love of God

For God so loved the world that He gave His one and only son. John 3:16

Charles C. Cooke

75

1. The love of God re-vealed in Je-sus, sent from a-bove to re-deem us from sin. The Bless-ed One, ho-ly and right-eous, o-pened the gates that we might en-ter in. Love so di-vine, the love of Je-sus poured out on Cal-va-ry's hill to save us.

2. The Word of God be-came in-car-nate to give our cap-tive hearts fi-nal re-lease. Free from the chains that was our es-tate in-to the realm of His con-quer-ing peace. Be-hold the King who reigns in glo-ry! Hum-bly we of-fer our prais-es to Thee.

WICKLOW
9.10.9.10.9.10.

76

Once for All for All of Us

I have brought You glory on earth by completing
the work You gave Me to do. John 17: 4
For Christ died for sins once for all... I Pet. 3:18

Charles C. Cooke

Moderato ♩ = 70

1. Once for all for all of us, Je-sus made the cross His own. On Gol-go-tha's
2. What com-mit-ment to be-hold to the Fa-ther's plan to save! To the end, the
3. Cov-ered with e-ter-nal grace, what a gift so full, so free! All for us to
4. Once for all for all of us, our sal-va-tion is com-plete. Man-i-fest-ed

dark-ened space ev-'ry earth-ly sin was strewn. "It is fin-ished!"
Lord o-beyed ev-en to the bit-ter grave. No-thing un-ful-
now em-brace! Ne'er a-gain sin's pov-er-ty shall in-trude or
by His blood, see His pierc-ed hands and feet! Love no hu-man

was His cry, then the King of kings would die.
filled re-mained, vic-to-ry the King has claimed.
wield its pow'r! Christ's great work o'er-comes this hour.
heart could know, God in heav'n came down to show.

WELCHMAN HALL
7.7.7.7.7.7.

O Christ, The First and Last

77

For God so loved the world that He gave His one and only Son... John 3:16

Arthur E. Smith

Charles C. Cooke

Moderato ♩ = 80

1. O Christ, the first and last, reign on for - ev - er - more. Your
2. O God, You loved the world and gave to hu - man race Your

reign all reigns out - last Your Lord-ship we a - dore. Your
Son, the Liv - ing Word, to die in sin - ner's place. All

king - dom knows no end be___ it ere time be - gan. Your
who in Christ be - lieves with___ Him will live and reign. His

rule, all rules trans - cend. What bless - ed news_ for man!
bless - ings to re - ceive when He shall come a - gain!

WILDEY
6.6.6.6.D.

78

Just Give Me Jesus

To me, to live is Christ. Phil. 1:21

Moderato ♩ = 86

Charles C. Cooke

1. Just give me Jesus, Lord, may I be champ-ioned in Your way? To
2. Just give me Jesus, Bless-ed King, You died to set me free. Up-
3. "Just give me Jesus", ere my cry, each tri - al I re - trace. Your

fol - low in the path You trod and learn to watch and pray? Lord,
on the cross each nail drove home my new-found des - ti - ny. One
guid - ing Hand in lead - ing me with un - sur - pass - ing grace. E -

may the grace re - leased in me be prompt-ing my re - sponse. To
pur - chased with Your prec - ious blood, pre - pared for me the way. The
quipped and ar - moured with Your word to ov - er - come life's snares, I

MILDRED
8.6.8.6.D.

love and_ serve; o - bey Your will; Lord, may I fail not once!
rich - es_ of_ the un - i - verse for not one drop could pay.
am as - sured and com - for - ted be - cause my Je - sus cares.

Fill Us, Fill Us With Thy Grace

79

... be filled with all the fullness of God. Eph. 3:19 (NKJV)

Charles C. Cooke

Moderato ♩ = 88

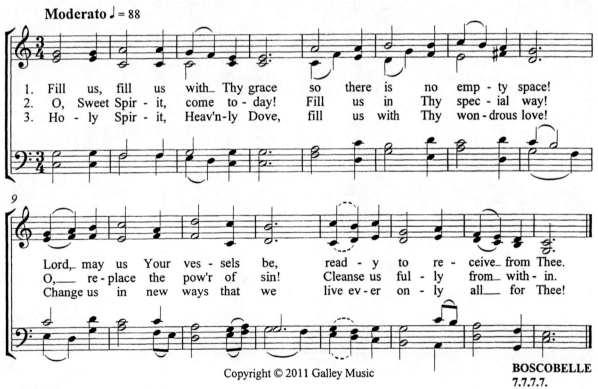

1. Fill us, fill us with_ Thy grace so there is no emp - ty space!
2. O, Sweet Spir - it, come to - day! Fill us in Thy spec - ial way!
3. Ho - ly Spir - it, Heav'n-ly Dove, fill us with Thy won - drous love!

Lord,_ may us Your ves - sels be, read - y to re - ceive_ from Thee.
O,_ re - place the pow'r of sin! Cleanse us ful - ly from_ with - in.
Change us in new ways that we live ev - er on - ly all_ for Thee!

BOSCOBELLE
7.7.7.7.

80 O Spirit of God Who Dwells Within

...you yourselves are God's temple...God's Spirit lives in you. 1 Cor. 3:16

Charles C. Cooke

Moderato ♩ = 78

1. O__ Spir-it of God who dwells with-in con-vict-ing__ pres-ence for all sin. For__
2. O__ Spir-it of God re-veal-ing Christ who paid the__ awe-some sa-cri-fice. The__
3. O__ Spir-it of God who judged the world up-on which Sa-tan's darts un-furled; for__
4. O__ Spir-it of God who guid-eth me in hol-i-ness and truth to see each

those who__ have a con-trite heart He will not__ e'er de-part. To
Sav-iour__ of a fall-en race He took our__ hope-less place. So
Christ that__ day on Cal-va-ry pro-claimed His__ vic-to-ry. A
form-ing__ thought and word and deed be min-is-tered by Thee. Trans-

us the__ Com-fort-er has__ come God breath-ing__ life a-new in
now with__ bold, en-light-ened minds His Lord-ship__ we re-ceive re-
vic-to-ry that now is__ mine the won-drous news to tell. The__
form-ing__ Spir-it take con-trol, this is my__ heart's de-sire. When

IRA
8.8.8.6.8.6.8.6.

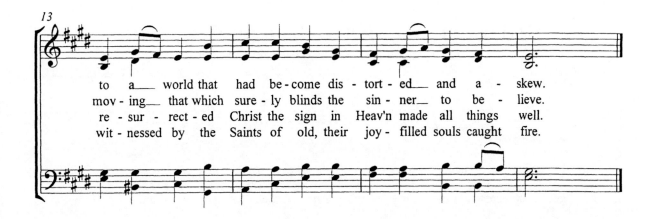

to a___ world that had be-come dis - tort - ed___ and a___ skew.
mov - ing___ that which sure - ly blinds the sin - ner___ to be - lieve.
re - sur - rect - ed Christ the sign in Heav'n made all things well.
wit - nessed by the Saints of old, their joy - filled souls caught fire.

Come, Gracious Spirit, Fill My Soul

Be filled with the Spirit. Eph. 5:18

81

Moderato ♩ = 80

Charles C. Cooke

1. Come, Gra - cious Spir - it fill my___ soul with fruit so I may move in
2. Ig - nite the___ flame to burn for___ Thee in ser - vice and in love. Con -
3. Trans - form the___ oft un - will - ing___ heart to trust as Thou wouldst lead and
4. Come, Gra - cious Spir - it, fill my___ soul with ev - er - last - ing praise of -

con - cert___ with Thy heav'n - ly___ role con - vict - ing___ to___ im - prove.
sum - ing___ fire of min - is - try com - mis - sioned from a - bove.
nur - ture___ all Thou dost im - part as life - sus - tain - ing seed.
fered to___ Thee not part but___ whole sweet in - cense all___ my days.

GRATE'S COVE
C.M.

82 Redeemer, You Have Brought Me Light

In Him we have redemption through His blood... Eph. 1:7a

Charles C. Cooke

1. Re - deem-er, You have brought me light. The dark-ness You ex - posed was
2. The val - leys of des - pair can quell the cheer - y heart with gloom un -
3. The em - bers of the fire took flame, a - wak - en - ing a -new my

all my life has ev - er known through all the steps I chose. But
less Christ is the cor - ner - stone, the Light that fills each room. What
one de - sire from deep with - in, O God, of ser - ving You. Em -

You re - vealed a - noth - er way paved with the gift of grace, where
joy could I re - count with tears which ov - er - whelmed my soul? The
bold - ened now with fer - vent hope to make the mes - sage known: The

ROSALIND JONES
C.M.D.

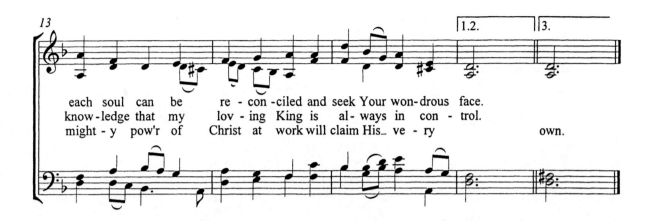

each soul can be re - con -ciled and seek Your won-drous face.
know-ledge that my lov - ing King is al- ways in con - trol.
might - y pow'r of Christ at work will claim His ve - ry own.

Save Us, O Lord, Our God

Save us, O Lord, our God... Psalm 106:47

83

Charles C. Cooke

Moderato ♩ = 90

1. Save us, O Lord,___ our God and ga -ther us up from the na-tions that
2. Save us, O Lord, for Christ's sake con - form-ing us all in His im-age that
3. Save us, O Lord, from our - selves en - light-en our hearts to be ho - ly that

we may give thanks to Your Ho - ly name and glo - ry in Your praise.
we are im-mersed in His ho - li - ness and count-ed a - mong the blest.
we may live lives with in - teg - ri - ty with wor-ship and praise for Thee.

WILFRED ARTHUR
Irregular Meter

84 Only God Can Save!

Salvation is found in no one else... Acts 4:12

Charles C. Cooke

1. My soul has found the sunlight where darkness and despair had once prevailed until assailed by Truth and Right. The Word of God revealing its pow'r to change and give the troubled one, the lost and 'lone the way to live.

2. The chosen tribe of Israel, they wandered o'er the years in desert land forsook the Hand that calmed their fears. The Law to them was given to follow and obey but they defied and then they tried to live their way.

3. A friend is found in Jesus, God's own Anointed Son. He paid the price, the sacrifice for ev'ry one. The love of God proclaiming the vic-t'ry over sin, who-e'er believes attains the keys to heav'n through Him.

Refrain
Sinking down to the depths of sin, only God can save! Only God can save!

ST. TIMOTHY'S AGINCOURT
Irregular meter

He who cleans-es__ from with-in, *(sing it!)* on-ly God__ can save! On-ly Him!

Never Go Hungry

85

*Then Jesus declared, "I am the Bread of Life. He who comes to me will
never go hungry, and he who believes in me will never be thirsty". John 6: 35*

Charles C. Cooke

Moderato ♩ = 70

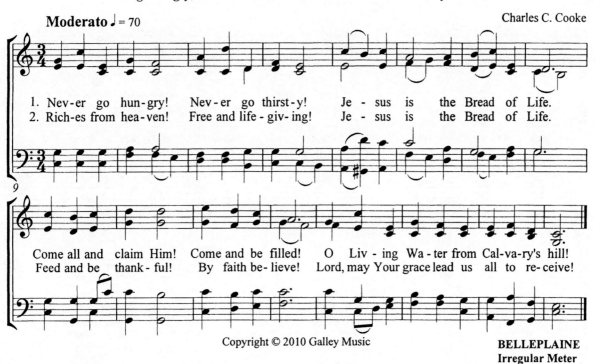

1. Nev-er go hun-gry! Nev-er go thirst-y! Je - sus is the Bread of Life.
2. Rich-es from hea-ven! Free and life-giv-ing! Je - sus is the Bread of Life.

Come all and claim Him! Come and be filled! O Liv - ing Wa-ter from Cal-va-ry's hill!
Feed and be thank-ful! By faith be-lieve! Lord, may Your grace lead us all to re-ceive!

BELLEPLAINE
Irregular Meter

86   Healing Flows

...one of the soldiers pierced Jesus' side with a spear,
bringing a sudden flow of blood and water. John 19:34

Charles C. Cooke

Moderato ♩ = 60

1. Heal-ing flows from the nail-pierced hands of Je - sus. Heal-ing flows from His
2. O, be washed in the cleans-ing stream from hea - ven! Sin's great debt is no
3. Love as wide as the out-stretched arms of Je - sus, in - fin - ite in its
4. Make us whole in our spir - it, soul and bo - dy! Make us whole from our

spear - pierced side. Heal - ing flows from the Lamb vic -
long - er owed! Sanc - ti - fied and made pure and
reach and span. Love so deep that the deep - est
brok - en ways! Make us whole and pre - sent us

tor - ious Healing flows from Christ cru - ci - fied.
blame - less through the wa - ter and blood that flowed!
o - cean seems as shal - low e - nough to stand.
ho - ly! Make us whole all our pil - grim days!

ROBIN BLUE
11.8.9.8.

Thy Healing Power Is Always Near

87

You anoint my head with oil... Psalm 23:5

Charles C. Cooke

Moderato ♩ = 80

1. Thy heal-ing pow'r is__ al-ways near at hand and sur-round ing__ me. A-
2. Thy heal-ing grace poured out on me, it cov-ers the seen, un-seen. Thy
3. Thy heal-ing blood on__ Cal-va-ry saved me from the dark a-byss. And
4. Thy Ho-ly Spir-it__ will a-noint the heart that is giv'n to__ Him and
5. Lord, con-se-crate my__ life to Thee in Thy ho-ly pres-ence now. O,

noint-ing oil up-on my head draws me clos-er__ un-to Thee.
mer-cies flow, O__ Lord, to me like an end-less liv-ing stream.
now my head a-waits the crown sig-ni-fy-ing heav'n-ly bliss.
bring the change that__ is de-sired: ho-li-ness long__ sought with-in.
no-thing more will__ I con-ceal 'tis my one and__ sol-emn vow.

Copyright © 2008 Galley Music

RHODODENDRON
8.7.8.7.

Lord, Son of David

88

Text: Matt. 20:31

Charles C. Cooke

Moderato ♩ = 70

"Lord, Son of Da-vid, have mer-cy on us!"

Copyright © 2010 Galley Music

89 Saviour, When I Am Uncertain

Vindicate me, O God, and plead my cause against an ungodly nation; Psalm 43:1a

Charles C. Cooke

Moderato ♩ = 84

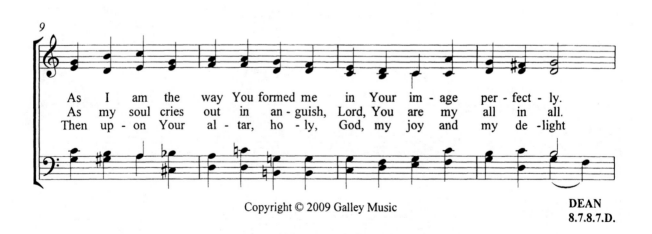

1. Sav-iour, when I am un-cer-tain, let me cling to You a-lone!
2. Tem-per my re-sponse to tor-ment with a Christ-like love to show!
3. Vin-di-cate me, Lord, my Sav-iour! Thus my prayer will al-ways be.

Turn me not from truth and wis-dom, make them now my cor-ner-stone!
Nev-er once, not for a mo-ment, should my coun-te-nance but glow.
Let Your light on me find fav-our shin-ing forth and dark-ness flee!

As I am the way You formed me in Your im-age per-fect-ly.
As my soul cries out in an-guish, Lord, You are my all in all.
Then up-on Your al-tar, ho-ly, God, my joy and my de-light

DEAN
8.7.8.7.D.

Yea, the lone - ly path be - fore me, I will tread with dig - ni - ty.
Use this ves - sel to ac - com - plish Your great will a - mong us all.
I will praise with soul and bo - dy end - less - ly both day and night.

Remember Me With Favour

90

Text: Neh. 13:31

Charles C. Cooke

Moderato ♩ = 70

Re - mem - ber me with fa - vour, O my God. Re -

mem - ber me with fa - vour, O my God.

91   Fear The Lord and Turn Away

Do not be wise in your own eyes; fear the Lord and shun evil. Prov. 3:7

Charles C. Cooke

Moderato ♩ = 80

1. Fear the Lord and turn a - way from e - vils that per - vade and roam.
2. Fear the Lord and add to life the bless - ings He will bring to sight!
3. Fear the Lord and He will grant the wis - dom to com - plete His will.

God is still your help and stay a for - tress for the home. For
Leave be - hind all woe and strife, em - brac - ing truth and right. For
World - ly ways He will sup - plant with heav'n - ly forms that fill. A

lo, the temp - ter is at work to cause your heart to sin. Lean
e - vil deeds are gain - less toil that on - ly count for loss un -
great - er un - der - stand - ing waits for those who seek the Lord. And

Copyright © 2008 Galley Music

FRERE PILGRIM
7.8.7.6.8.6.8.6.

on the Rock to re - as - sert your strength. O, look to Him!
less the sin - ner claims the soil be - neath Cal - va - ry's cross.
on His Word who med - i - tates will find His sweet ac - cord.

In the Here and Now

Then the Lord said to him, "What is that in your hand?". Ex. 4:2

Charles C. Cooke

92

Moderato ♩ = 80

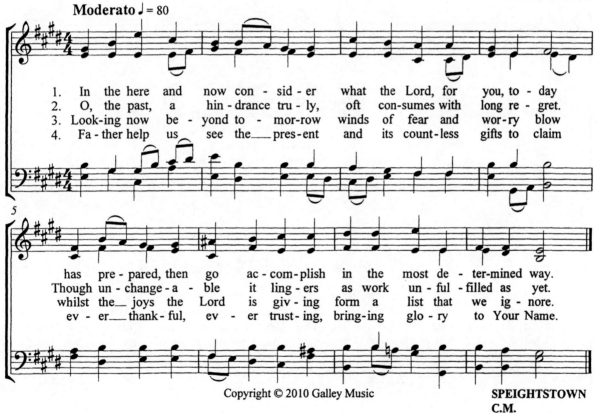

1. In the here and now con - sid - er what the Lord, for you, to - day
2. O, the past, a hin - drance tru - ly, oft con - sumes with long re - gret.
3. Look-ing now be - yond to - mor-row winds of fear and wor - ry blow
4. Fa - ther help us see the pres-ent and its count-less gifts to claim

has pre - pared, then go ac - com-plish in the most de - ter-mined way.
Though un - change - a - ble it ling - ers as work un - ful - filled as yet.
whilst the joys the Lord is giv - ing form a list that we ig - nore.
ev - er thank - ful, ev - er trust-ing, bring-ing glo - ry to Your Name.

Copyright © 2010 Galley Music

SPEIGHTSTOWN
C.M.

93 We All Need Christian Fellowship

Let us not give up meeting together... but let us encourage one another... Heb. 10:25

Charles C. Cooke

Moderato ♩ = 90

1. We all need Christ-ian fel-low-ship to bind our hearts as one in
2. En - cour-age one an - oth - er with the Word con - tin - ual - ly. Ex-
3. Our in - ter-ced - ing eff - orts bring re - wards we oft - en see. Our
4. Sup - port from our church fam - i - ly brings u - ni - fy - ing joy. The

Je - sus who taught us to love e'en those un - known. So
alt - ing, not fault - ing then most as - sur - ed - ly we'll
bro - thers and sis - ters re - joice in psalm - o - dy. They
kin - ship in wor - ship which bo - dy, soul em - ploy de -

lift each oth - er up in prayer and let your ser - vice be to
find good fa - vour with the One who brought us from our sin and
praise the Lord with wit - ness - ing what He has done for them. Their
lights the Lord whose per - fect plan is our sweet har - mo - ny. Then

ST. JOHN'S
8.6.6.6.8.6.8.6.

com-fort lost, af - flict - ed souls in their in - fir - mi - ty.
taught us how to care for oth - ers as if_ un - to Him.
Lord and Mas - ter, Gra-cious King, Blest Sav - iour,_what a Friend!
may the peace of Christ be ours, O Lord, so_ let it be!

Undo the Trespass I Commit

94

Peter went out and wept bitterly. Luke 22:62 (NKJV)

Charles C. Cooke

Moderato ♩ = 75

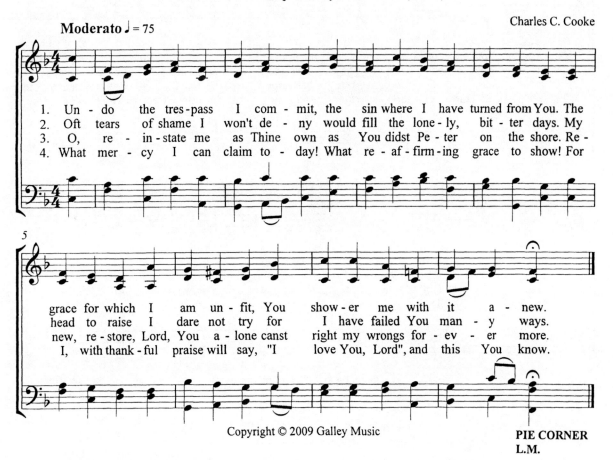

1. Un - do the tres-pass I com - mit, the sin where I have turned from You. The
2. Oft tears of shame I won't de - ny would fill the lone - ly, bit - ter days. My
3. O, re - in-state me as Thine own as You didst Pe - ter on the shore. Re -
4. What mer - cy I can claim to - day! What re - af - firm-ing grace to show! For

grace for which I am un - fit, You show - er me with it a - new.
head to raise I dare not try for I have failed You man - y ways.
new, re - store, Lord, You a - lone canst right my wrongs for - ev - er more.
I, with thank - ful praise will say, "I love You, Lord", and this You know.

PIE CORNER
L.M.

95

Go and Be Reconciled

For if you forgive men when they sin against you,
your heavenly Father will also forgive you. Matt. 6:14

Charles C. Cooke

Andante ♩ = 80

1. Go and be re-con-ciled. Go to your broth-er. Let not one an-gry word
2. Be right be-fore His eyes! Step out in bold-ness! O, let your broth-er's hand
3. We were a fall-en race doomed through con-vict-ion if God had turned His face
4. For-give us, Lord, we pray each time we fal-ter. Spir-it, show us the way

fol-low an-oth-er! You were cre-a-ted in the im-age of our
bring warmth to cold-ness! May har-mo-ny and peace be the on-ly way a-
from our af-flict-ion. But Christ was sac-ri-ficed, an a-tone-ment for our
back to Thine al-tar! Have mer-cy on us now through Thy re-con-cil-ing

God. Go and be re-con-ciled in the name of Love.
head. God grant-eth sweet re-lease. Seek Him and be led!
sin. God re-con-ciled the way, brought us back to Him.
pow'r! This is our sol-emn prayer made this ve-ry hour.

LINDEN
6.5.6.5.7.7.6.5.

Do Not Be Weary

96

Let us not become weary in doing good... Gal. 6:9

Charles C. Cooke

Moderato ♩ = 90

1. Do not be wea-ry in do-ing good for you will
2. Car-ry the bur-den of some-one else! Let your com-
3. Be-come the sow-er of the good seed through-out the

reap your re - ward._____ To all the peo - ple,
pass - ion shine through!_____ Mo - del Christ's teach - ing
na - tions for Him!_____ His pow'r will nur - ture

all the be - liev - ers: O, learn the works of the Lord!_____
of be - ing self - less! Show them what pure love can do!_____
and bring to flow - er all of the beau - ty with - in._____

ENID
5.4.7.5.5.7.

97 My Burden Grows Lighter

Come to Me, all who are weary and burdened and I will give you rest. Matt. 11:28

Charles C. Cooke

Moderato ♩ = 90

1. My bur - den grows light - er and light - er ev - 'ry day.___ His
2. The yoke of Christ is eas - y. He will not let me bear___ a
3. He gives aid to___ the wear - y and strength - ens the weak.___ And
4. With arms up - raised to hea - ven I know He walks be - side,___ re -

Light___ glows___ bright - er and bright - er on my way to
bur - den far be - yond me or cause me to des - pair. For
those who hope know clear - ly they'll reach the high - est peak. And
mov - ing ev - 'ry bur - den when doubt and woe be - tide. O

know - ing Him and___ trust - ing His prom - is - es, I'm blessed. And
He has great com - pas - sion and knows the se - cret place of
soar on wings like___ eag - les with strength re - newed and then all
for to dwell in___ safe - ty and shel - tered all day long! He

BRENTCLIFF
7.6.7.6.D.

see my life__ ad - just - ing and seek - ing His sweet rest.
each one of__ His child - ren and cov - ers it with grace.
na - tions and__ all peo - ples may see and fol - low Him.
is my Lord__ who bears me and He who makes me strong.

There Is Always Room at the Cross 98

Come to Me, all you who are weary and burdened, and I will give you rest. Matt. 11:28

Charles C. Cooke

Moderato ♩ = 70

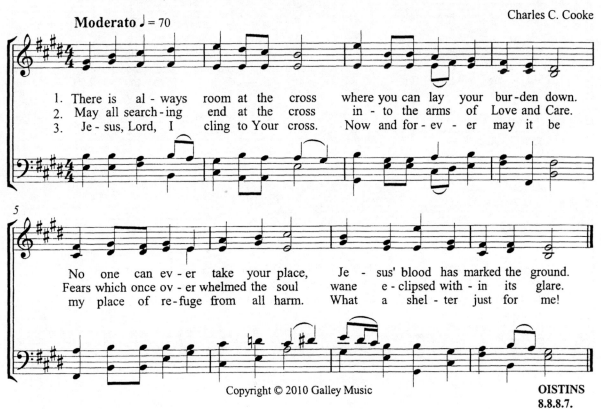

1. There is al - ways room at the cross where you can lay your bur-den down.
2. May all search-ing end at the cross in - to the arms of Love and Care.
3. Je - sus, Lord, I cling to Your cross. Now and for - ev - er may it be

No one can ev - er take your place, Je - sus' blood has marked the ground.
Fears which once ov - er whelmed the soul wane e - clipsed with - in its glare.
my place of re - fuge from all harm. What a shel - ter just for me!

OISTINS
8.8.8.7.

99   When Two Are Joined in Perfect Love

"Therefore what God has joined together, let man not separate". Mark 10:9

Charles C. Cooke

Moderato ♩ = 80

1. When two are joined in per - fect love, Your Name, O Lord we__ praise. For
2. U - nit - ed and no long - er two be - fore the sight of__ God. A
3. This per - fect gift en - rich - es all and builds the bod - y__ well. Up -

vows are shared with deep re - solve to last through - out their years. We
new cre - a - tion go - ing forth with beau - ty and un - flawed! To
hold - ing with in - teg - ri - ty a ho - ly love to tell. As

wit - ness that com - mit - ment__ made be - fore Your throne of grace. Of
face the world as tri - als__ come, our firm sup - port we give. We
to - kens are ex - changed, O__ Lord, re - new our faith we pray. That

BRERETON
C.M.D.

13

hopes and dreams to nev - er___ fade from that first warm em - brace.
pray, O Lord, Your bless - ings_ flow up - on them as they live.
as be - liev - ers we will_ be Your bride that joy - ful day!

Give Thanks to the Lord

100

Text: 2 Chron. 20:21

Charles C. Cooke

Moderato ♩ = 70

Give thanks to the Lord for His love en - dures for__ ev - er.

101 Bring Your Gifts to God, the Father!

Bring the whole tithe into the storehouse... Mal. 3:10a

Charles C. Cooke

Moderato ♩ = 90

1. Bring your gifts to God, the__ Fa-ther! Bring your. pres-ents__ oft to__ Him!
2. God has__ giv-en us do-min-ion o'er the__ land and__ sea to__ show
3. May our__ lives which we hold__ dear-est be our__ one most pre-cious gift

May the__ tithe of all you ga-ther be a__ grate-ful of-fer-ing.
His pro-vis-ion for His__ child-ren. There is__ noth-ing__ we fore-go.
Of-fered up to Him, the__ Fair-est, ev-'ry__ form of__ praise we lift.

God, the__ Giv-er, like__ no oth-er knows our__ needs be-fore__ we__ know.
We must do His work__ with fer-vour us-ing His re-sour-ces__ well.
God has__ saved us through Lord Je-sus. We were lost but now__ are__ found.

EBONY DRIVE
8.7.8.7.D.

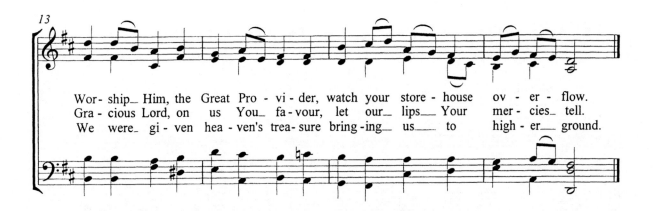

Worship Him, the Great Pro - vi - der, watch your store - house ov - er - flow.
Gra - cious Lord, on us You fa - vour, let our lips Your mer - cies tell.
We were gi - ven hea - ven's trea - sure bring - ing us to high - er ground.

More of Jesus I Would Want

Whether we live or die, we belong to the Lord. Rom 14:8

Charles C. Cooke

Moderato ♩ = 70

1. More of Je - sus I would want. More of Him would then sup - plant
2. More to Je - sus I must give. More for Him now I must live.
3. More in Je - sus I must grow. More of Him to get to know.

my fu - tile bat - tle 'gainst all sin; find - ing vic - to - ry with Him.
Rea - dy for ser - vice to ful - fill all re - veal - ings of His will.
His word to trea - sure in my heart know - ing - ly to then im - part.

RIVER BAY
7.7.8.7.

103 Grant Us Wisdom In Abundance

For the Lord gives wisdom, and from His mouth come knowledge and understanding. Prov. 2:6

Moderato ♩ = 88
Descant last stanza

Charles C. Cooke

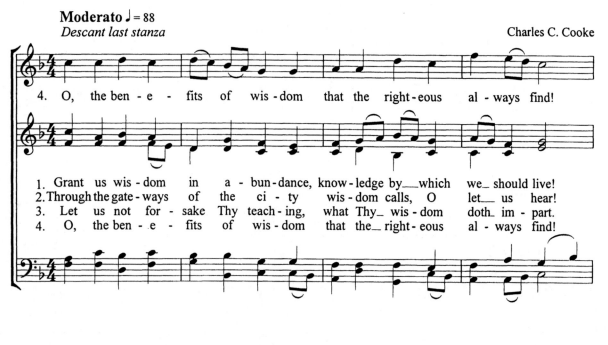

4. O, the ben-e-fits of wis-dom that the right-eous al-ways find!

1. Grant us wis-dom in a-bun-dance, know-ledge by__which we__ should live!
2. Through the gate-ways of the ci-ty wis-dom calls, O let__ us hear!
3. Let us not for-sake Thy teach-ing, what Thy__ wis-dom doth__ im-part.
4. O, the ben-e-fits of wis-dom that the__ right-eous al-ways find!

Liv-ing life for God's__ great__ king-dom, first__ and__ fore-most on the mind!

Give us words so filled with sub-stance that the__world can nev-er give!
Rouse our slum-ber of self-pi-ty with an__ ev-er lis-t'ning ear!
Truth that's al-ways ev-er reach-ing for the__ un-der-stand-ing heart!
Liv-ing life for God's great king-dom, first and__ fore-most on the mind!

CHRISTOPHER
8.7.8.7.D.

9

Lord, with thank-ful hearts we praise Thee,_ giv - ing_ hon - our_ to Thy Name.

When we_ speak, let there be_ pow - er, Lord, with_ grace and grav - i - ty.
As we_ seek this hid - den treas - ure, Lord we_ come in rev 'rent_ fear.
He who_ walks with great dis - cret - ion is pro - tect - ed from the_ snare
Lord, with_ thank - ful hearts we_ praise Thee, giv - ing_ hon - our to Thy_ Name.

13

We are blessed for in_ Thy_ mer - cy, wis - dom know-ledge we may claim.

Like a gar - den's sweet - est flow - er, give us words per - fumed with Thee!
Grant us wis - dom in Thy meas - ure! This is our most hum - ble prayer.
lurk - ing for to take pos - ses - sion of the sim - ple, un - a - ware.
We are blessed for in Thy mer - cy, wis - dom know-ledge we may claim.

104 Let Those Who Serve Be Counted

Let the elders who direct the affairs of the church well
are worthy of double honour... 1 Tim. 5:17

Charles C. Cooke

Moderato ♩ = 90

1. Let those who serve be count - ed and giv - en hon - our too. The
2. The ded - i - ca - ted lead - ers are sol - diers in the fight to
3. The el - ders who di - rect_ the church bring glo - ry un - to God. They
4. They're shep-herds of God's prec - ious flock that thrives un - der their care. and
5. All praise and thanks to God,_ Most High, for call - ing those who lead. For

faith - ful ones who teach_ the Word and spur our souls a - new. With
ga - ther all be - liev - ers and bring them to the Light. With
give to those who seek_ and search new hope through Christ the Lord. Their
look to Him the Stead - fast Rock to guide and ov - er - seer. Not
Thee they live to glo - ri - fy through help - ing those in need. We

fer - vour_ for the king - dom goals re - spond - ing to the call, they
ar - mour_ of the Liv - ing God their bod - ies are be - clothed with
sweet re - ward is life trans-formed for those once count - ed lost are
for the_ hope of sel - fish gain but eag - er - ness to bring the
lift them, Lord, to Thee in prayer may Thy sus - tain - ing grace sur -

MAXWELL ROAD
8.6.8.6.D.

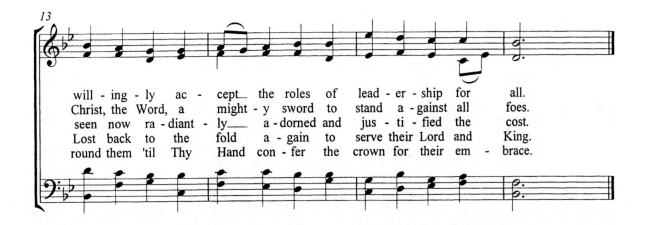

will - ing - ly ac - cept the roles of lead - er - ship for all.
Christ, the Word, a might - y sword to stand a - gainst all foes.
seen now ra - diant - ly a - dorned and jus - ti - fied the cost.
Lost back to the fold a - gain to serve their Lord and King.
round them 'til Thy Hand con - fer the crown for their em - brace.

What Fleeting Praise We Often Seek! 105

"Be careful not to do your 'acts of righteousness' before men, to be seen by them". Matt. 6:1

Charles C. Cooke

Maestoso ♩ = 70

1. What fleet-ing praise we oft - en seek! Sweet are the mouths that flat - ter! But
2. When giv-ing no one else should know, not e'en the hand be - side us. For
3. When pray-ing find a clos - et space be - yond the world's in - tru - sion! Let
4. When fast-ing may our joy shine through a coun - te - nance su - per - nal! At -

God re - quires a se - cret place for all good works that mat - ter.
God in hea - ven knows the heart and o - pen - ly will bless us.
our sur - ren - der be en - clothed in bless - ed sweet com - mun - ion!
tuned com - plete - ly to the Lord our rad - iance is e - ter - nal!

Copyright © 2011 Galley Music

MANILA
8.7.8.7.

106

Are You Ready?
(The Lord Has A Mission for Each One on the Earth)

... for God's gifts and His call are irrevocable. Rom. 11:29

Charles C. Cooke

Moderato ♩ = 85

1. The Lord has a mis - sion for each one on the earth that He has de - ter - mined be -
2. His Spir - it will guide_ you pre - par-ing you to serve and there-by re - veal - ing your
3. O, an -swer His call - ing it does-n't mat-ter where! Be set for the jour - ney, your

fore our ve - ry birth. May hearts now be op - en and there for Him to fill; con -
deep un-known re-serves. You will not be wea - ry. His prom-is - es you know when
wait-ing heart pre - pare! The wave - flow of pass - ion will soon en - gulf your soul. As

Refrain

formed to and do - ing His will.
He calls your name_ and says "Go"! Are you read-y for the task should the Sav-iour ask? Are you
you are em-pow - ered, be bold!

read - y for the task at hand?_____ When His eyes roam to and fro look-ing

ARE YOU READY
Irregular Meter

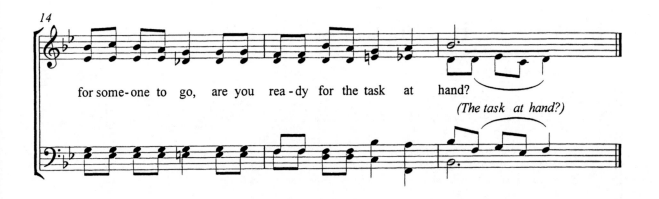

for some-one to go, are you rea-dy for the task at hand?

(The task at hand?)

I Have Heard of You

107

Text: Job 42:5 (NKJV)

Charles C. Cooke

Moderato ♩ = 70

I have heard___ of You by the hear-ing of the ear. I have

heard___ of You by the hear-ing of the ear.

108 Lord, Hear the Cry of Those Who Dwell

I will also gather all nations, and bring them down into the Valley of Jehoshaphat... Joel 3:2a

Moderato ♩ = 90

Charles C. Cooke

1. Lord, hear the cry of__ those who dwell a - midst the din of pro - gress whose
2. The thoughts of some are__ oft con - strained with - in a dark per - cept - ion that
3. Lord, may we e'er be__ prais - ing Thee each day up - on our ris - ing. Let

one de - sire is__ to re - tell their stor - ies and bear wit - ness. O,
life be - yond this__ fin - ite plane is on - ly mis - con - cept - ion. But
thanks con - sume our__ rev - er - ie with qui - et joy a - bid - ing! For

that these truths be giv - en__ voice with pow - er and ex - press - ion, that
those who trust the Liv - ing__ Word can tell the awe - some sto - ry. They
hope is our e - ter - nal__ quest its in - cense sweet to sav - our, lies

those who hear would claim the choice of Je - sus__ and His mis - sion.
have a home with__ Christ, the Lord, a heav'n - ly__ home in glo - ry.
in our faith when we con - fess Lord Je - sus__ Christ as Sav - iour.

NYEMYA-OMBE
8.7.8.7.D

Lord, The Fields Are White For Harvest   109

... lift up your eyes and look at the fields, for they are already white for harvest! John 4:35b (NKJV)

Charles C. Cooke
Last stanza descant by Jason D. Locke

Moderato ♩ = 90

Descant Last stanza

5. Have Your way as I move forward armed with an un-sha-ken faith

1. Lord, the fields are white for har-vest will-ing work-ers are but few,
2. Peo-ple in their in-most be-ing need to know they're saved by grace,
3. Lead me to a life of ser-vice, God, for You, my all I give.
4. Teach me how to love my bro-ther though in dis-tant land may be,
5. Have Your way as I move for-ward armed with an un-sha-ken faith.

May Your truth, as I look heav'n-ward re-son-ate through ev-'ry race.

move my heart to pla-ces far-thest from the com-fort of my pew.
may their yearn-ing, may their long-ing find in You a rest-ing place.
Help me to ful-fil the prom-ise birthed in me each day I live,
reach a-cross and help a-no-ther share what You have gi-ven me.
May Your truth, as I look heav'n-ward re-son-ate through ev-'ry race.

SAULT STE. MARIE
8.7.8.7.

110 Open My Eyes Lord

"... whatever you did for one of the least of these brothers of mine you did it for Me". Matt. 25:40b

Charles C. Cooke

Moderato ♩ = 80

1. O - pen my eyes, Lord let me__ see the press - ing need sur -
2. O - pen my ears, Lord let me__ hear the cries of those who
3. O - pen my mouth, Lord let me__ speak the truth of the neg -
4. O - pen my heart, Lord let me__ feel the love that Thou didst
5. Dis - pel all fear of those un - known to claim a world out -

round - ing__ me. When all seems_ lost and thus con - fine the
feel des - pair. May I bring_ help that will suc - ceed, not
lect - ed,__ weak. May I give_ voice where none ex - ist to
not con - ceal to lift us__ from the mi - ry__ clay and
side my__ own. Let Thy Great_ Hand di - rect each_ task that

vis - ion__ of the troub - led mind, grant me a__ heart to
on - ly__ thought and word but deed. May pa - tience_ be the
right - ful__ caus - es and per - sist. Bless Thou the__ way to
gave us__ life a - new to - day. A love to__ share; a
I may__ yearn for more and ask! Let no self - in - t'rest

WORKMANS
8.8.8.8.8.8.

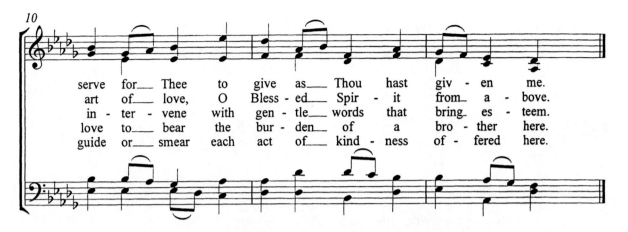

serve for___ Thee to give as___ Thou hast giv - en me.
art of___ love, O Bless - ed___ Spir - it from___ a - bove.
in - ter - vene with gen - tle___ words that bring_ es - teem.
love to___ bear the bur - den___ of a bro - ther here.
guide or___ smear each act of___ kind - ness of - fered here.

6. The more I love Thee, Lord may I
   Give love that always multiply.
   To have compassion for the poor
   And greet them with an open door.
   Let others' needs be mine instead,
   O Thou who gives us daily bread!

7. To care and love our fellow-man
   Is part of God's eternal plan.
   "For as you do it for the least
   You do it as if unto Me".
   All glory be to Thee, Most High!
   All thanks to Thee who doth supply!

Show Us the Better Way, O Lord

111

Charles C. Cooke

Moderato ♩ = 80

Show us the bet - ter way, O Lord. Re - di - rect us!

112 Every Day Is A Day Closer
(How Lovely is Your House, O Father!)

How lovely is Your dwelling place, O LORD Almighty! Psalm 84:1

Charles C. Cooke

Moderato ♩ = 90

1. How love - ly is Your House, O Fa - ther! How love - ly is Your dwell - ing place! Just one day in Your courts is bet - ter than
2. The prom - is - es the Lord has made me: He's faith - ful, He is just and true. The love that He be - stows com - plete - ly brought
3. He helps me to re - sist temp - ta - tion while tra - vel - ling life's dai - ly path. The goal of an as - sured sal - va - tion and
4. That day when with the saints re - joic - ing I'll meet my Sav - iour, Lord and King. With per - fect har - mo - ny and voic - ing I'll
5. A - las! I have a home in glo - ry where all the bright - est and the best gath - ered 'round the throne most ho - ly to

Copyright © 2007 Galley Music

ROSETTA
Irregular meter

Refrain

thou - sands with - out Your grace.
hope, brought me life a - new.
spared from His aw - ful wrath.
wor - ship and praise and sing.
claim their e - ter - nal rest.

O,

ev - 'ry day is a day clos-er clos-er to meet-ing my Lord.
(clos - er)

Ev -'ry day is a day clos-er, clos-er to meet-ing my Lord.

clos - er,

113

In His Care

You are my hiding place. Psalm 32:7a

Charles C. Cooke

Moderato ♩ = 94

1. In His care. When we all get to hea-ven we'll be in the glare of His
2. In His name, those who ask will most sure-ly re-ceive. We pro-claim, we af-
3. In His hands, we are com-for-ted, safe and se-cure. The de-mands of the

great maj-es-ty.____ to be-hold all the saints in the
firm, we be-lieve.____ What a Friend! What a Sav-iour whose
world are no more.____ Ho-ly one, we are wor-ship-ping

king-dom of Light who have fought, who have fought the good fight.____
love in-ter-cedes at the throne full of grace for our needs!____
there at Your feet. Hea-ven's own, our re-demp-tion com-plete!____

GWENYTH
12.9.12.9.11.10.

Dedicated to Pastor Dr. Robert Buchanan and Elaine Buchanan, Wesley Chapel Free Methodist Church, Toronto, Ontario

We will praise and wor-ship the Lord for - ev - er whose
We are blessed be - yond our im - ag - i - na - tion and
In that great, great ci - ty of souls re - joic - ing, our

grace re - deemed us from sin's dark - est night.
mer - it noth - ing for life - long mis - deeds.
song of praise will for - ev - er re - peat.

Consider the Great Love of the Lord 114

Charles C. Cooke

Moderato ♩ = 70

Con - si - der, con - si - der the great love of the Lord.

115 His Comfort Is Given to Those Who Grieve

God will wipe away every tear from their eyes. Rev. 7:17

Charles C. Cooke

Moderato ♩ = 80

1. His com - fort is giv'n to those_ who grieve. The pain_ of loss He will_ re - lieve. Each ful - some tear is wiped_ a - way, re - veal - ing now a bright - er day where all_ the saints in
2. For man - y who re - main_ be - hind so oft - en in their troub - led mind will ques - tion why their loved_ one left all swal - lowed by the throes of death. But Christ, the Lord, their
3. His per - fect peace is theirs_ to claim. The wound - ed spir - it calls_ His name for sweet_ re - pose, for sooth - ing balm, for stead - y streams of love_ and calm. The Lord_ of heav'n and
4. En - cour - age - ment and grace_ are sealed with - in_ His prom - is - es_ to heal. The bro - ken heart con - sumed by grief, the an - guished soul now finds_ re - lief. But Christ. who tri - umphed
5. Where pain_ and sor - row once_ were rife, the Sav - iour gives e - ter - nal life. This bless - ed Truth; this prec - ious gem; this fi - nal home: Je - ru - sa - lem. The rest - ing place where

COBIN HINDS
10.10.10.10.10.10.

19

glo - ry meet for - ev - er joy - ful and__ com - plete.
loved one now see for He__ has won the vic - to - ry.
earth__ gives hope and in - ner strength with which__ to cope.
o'er__ the tomb is Light - dis - pel - ling dark-ness and gloom.
all__ will meet in joy - filled wor - ship at__ His feet.

He Who Destroyed the Power of Death · 116

*... by His death He might break the power of him who holds the power of death...
and free those who...were held in slavery by their fear of death. Hebrews 2:14-15*

Charles C. Cooke

Andante ♩ = 85

1. He who des-troyed the pow'r of__death and drained the caul - dron of__ its__ fear, has
2. That sep - a - rat - ing pow'r of__death: im - pen - e - tra - ble as__ it's__ cold! En-
3. Though hearts are grieved and pain__ is__ rife, the word__ of God stands ev - er__ clear. In
4. Mourn not__ for those de - part - ed__souls for they__ are in His pres - ence__ near but

9

paved the way for our__ re - birth: a liv - ing branch with fruit__ to bear.
dure__ will we this tem - p'ral state un - til__ our King has made us whole!
the__sweet full - ness of__ His time, our God__ will wipe a - way__ each tear.
for__ the ones a - mong us still who know not of His love__ and care.

WRIGHT
L.M.

117 Great Peace Have Those Who Love Your Law

Great peace have those who love Your law , and nothing can make them stumble. Psalm 119:165

Charles C. Cooke

Moderato ♩ = 70

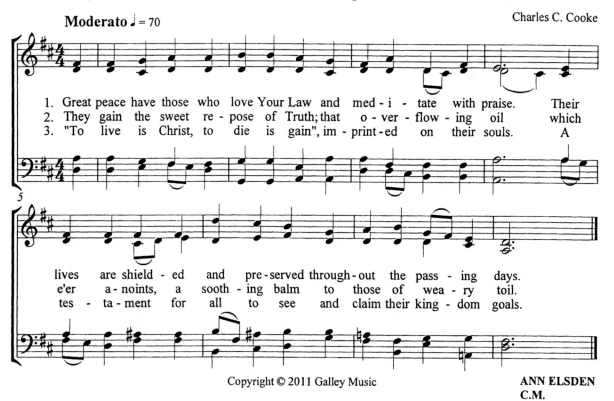

1. Great peace have those who love Your Law and med-i-tate with praise. Their
2. They gain the sweet re-pose of Truth; that o-ver-flow-ing oil which
3. "To live is Christ, to die is gain", im-print-ed on their souls. A

lives are shield-ed and pre-served through-out the pass-ing days.
e'er a-noints, a sooth-ing balm to those of wea-ry toil.
tes-ta-ment for all to see and claim their king-dom goals.

ANN ELSDEN
C.M.

118   I Am He

Text: Isaiah 46:4

Moderato ♩ = 70

Charles C. Cooke

I am He,_____ I am He who_ will sus-tain_ you.

The Eternal God Is Your Refuge

119

Text: Deut. 33:3, 27

Charles C. Cooke
Accomp. Arr.by Jason D. Locke

Andante ♩ = 60

Unison

The e - ter - nal God is your re - fuge___ and un - der- neath are the ev - er - last - ing arms. Sure - ly it is You who love the peo - ple;___ all the ho - ly ones are in Your hand.

FLAGSTAFF
Irregular Meter

120 Around The Throne of God

All the angels were standing around the throne and around the elders... Rev. 7:11

Charles C. Cooke

Moderato ♩ = 80

1. A - round the throne of God_____ with awe - filled eyes we stand. This
2. The ho - li - est of pla - ces where rev - er - ence a - bound. The
3. The heav'n - ly robes of light_____ in which we are be - clothed; with
4. As we a - wait this glo - ry to join the King of Love, this

is our one a - bid - ing hope to join His cho - sen band. With
an - gels hide their fa - ces stand - ing on sac - red ground. Re -
ra - di - ant re - splend - en - cy for bod - ies now trans - posed. The
earth - ly life should train our souls for serv - ing Him a - bove. Let

joy - ful praise our__ tongues de - light in wor - ship of the King. But
joic - ing as they__ serve the Lord, re - peat - ing their sweet song: "Ho -
Lord who reigns in__ maj - es - ty sur - round - ed by His bride has
wor - ship be the__ flame that burns with - in our thank - ful heart as

Copyright © 2008 Galley Music

CAMERON
8.6.8.6.D.

to des-cribe the awe- some sight to mind no words could bring.
ly, ho - ly, ho - ly", they laud with praise all the day long.
lov -ing - ly pre -pared the feast o'er which He will pre - side.
we look to e - ter - ni - ty to con - sum -mate our part.

How Long Have You Awaited, Lord? 121

... So they went out and got into the boat, but that night they caught nothing. John 21:3

Charles C. Cooke

Maestoso ♩ = 70

1. How long have You a - wait -ed Lord, while fool - ish hearts in vain have
2. Each night of un - re - ward -ed toil de - pletes the soul of cheer, but
3. O Grac- ious Lord, in us do make our flound-'ring ways to cease, a -

drift - ed from Your shore of love when to reach for You is gain?
morn- ing light re - veals a - new Your a - bun -dan - cy is near.
bid - ing in Your love by faith and to find Your bless - ed peace.

BATHSHEBA
8.6.8.7.

122 Life Beyond the Golden Sunset

"Now the dwelling of God is with men, and He will live with them..." Rev. 21:3

Moderato ♩ = 60

Charles C. Cooke

1. Life be-yond the gold-en sun-set past the reach of anx-ious toil:
2. Peace sur-rounds the soul for-ev-er. Per-fect peace at last to find.
3. Joy un-known and ne'er re-cord-ed through the course of ag-es past,

O, what beau-ty from the out-set, sweet with God's re-fresh-ing oil!
In the bos-om of the Sav-iour, gath-ered saints of ev-'ry kind!
fills the man-sions Christ ac-cord-ed to His faith-ful ones at last.

Bound-less is His place of dwell-ing for a-mong us He will reign.
O, that which was most e-lu-sive, pas-sion-ate-ly sought by all
Glor-ious bod-ies now like Je-sus, clothed in ev-er-last-ing light!

CHAPEL ROAD
8.7.8.7.D.

Match-less grace and love com-pel - ling, all a - vailed in His do - main!
now be-comes the realm ex - clu - sive un - to those who heed His call.
Re - u - ni - ted loves are joy - ous wit-ness-ing the awe - some sight!

Not Ours to Know

No one knows about that day or hour... Mark 13:32

Charles C. Cooke

123

Moderato ♩ = 74

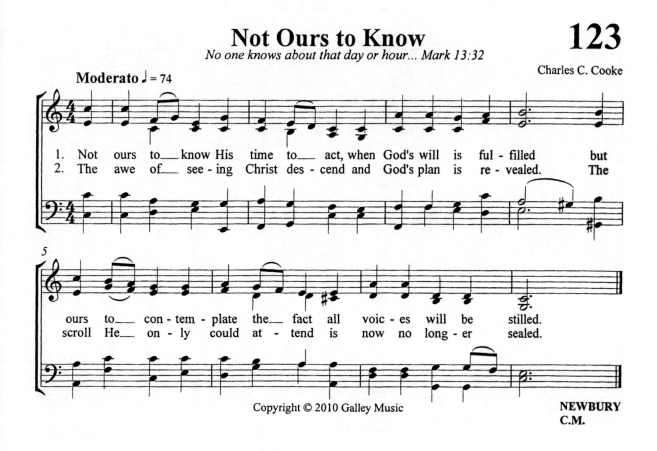

1. Not ours to know His time to act, when God's will is ful - filled but
2. The awe of see - ing Christ des - cend and God's plan is re - vealed. The

ours to con - tem - plate the fact all voic - es will be stilled.
scroll He on - ly could at - tend is now no long - er sealed.

NEWBURY
C.M.

124 Night Recedes Forevermore

There will be no more night. Rev. 22:5a

Charles C. Cooke

Moderato ♩ = 80

1. Night re-cedes for - ev - er-more | in the new Je - ru - sa - lem. | Dark-ness of the
2. Crys-tal wa - ter flow-ing down | in the new Je - ru - sa - lem | from God's great ma-
3. Tree of life now is re - vealed | in the new Je - ru - sa - lem. | Yield-ing fruit in
4. Lord, our God for - ev - er reigns | in the new Je - ru - sa - lem | where His ser-vants
5. Nev - er more to thirst a - gain | in the new Je - ru - sa - lem | where the gift of

world now past 'twill be light that lasts and lasts. Ev - er - last - ing
jes - tic throne to our now e - ter - nal home. All re-freshed with
seas - on well, heal - ing where the na - tions dwell! Blest are they whose
saved by grace bear His name up - on their face. Lo, the sun will
life is free in the wa - ter by the tree. Come, O come and

light we see. God in full re - splen - den - cy!
souls re - stored, bless - ed ser - vants of the Lord!
robes are white, they may claim the tree, their right!
seem as night when com - pared to God's pure light.
wor - ship Him: the Be - gin - ning and the End!

ROZANNE JONES
7.7.7.7.7.7

God's Rest for Which We Strive

125

Therefore since the promise of entering His rest still stands...
now we who have believed enter that rest... Heb. 4:1-3

Charles C. Cooke

Moderato ♩ = 90

1. God's rest for which we strive to en-ter and to dwell a-mong be-liev-ing souls His praise___ to tell. A prom-ise that has cap-tured hearts ere time be-gan with faith-ful-ness our spir-its know it's God's great plan.

2. A place of per-fect peace, its full-ness to ex-plore. Com-mun-ion with our God whom we___ a-dore! A glo-rious life of joy and ser-vice to our King, en-fold-ed in His love our thank-ful-ness we bring.

3. O-bed-i-ence and trust while liv-ing for the Lord! This meas-ure to at-tain: His sweet___ ac-cord! The nev-er end-ing state in glo-ry to a-bide, that lifts our souls for-ev-er stand-ing by His side.

PICO TENERIFE
6.6.6.4.12.12.

126 God Will Judge Each One

...and each person was judged according to what he had done. Rev. 20:13b

Moderato ♩ = 92

Charles C. Cooke

1. God will judge each one__ be - fore Him at the fin - al trum - pet call.
2. By our words we are__ ac - quit - ted. By our words we are__ con - demned.
3. He will bring the past__ be - fore us: an ac - count we all__ must give.
4. Our ful - fill - ing cloak of glo - ry is con - ferred at His__ com - mand

Saints and sin - ners bow__ be - fore Him and pro - claim Him Lord__ of all.
When our lives are firm - ly fit - ted in the ways He will__ com - mend,
Our o - be - di - ence__ to Je - sus; how it framed the way__ we lived.
when we live the Christ - ian sto - ry: love of God and fel - low man.

Then the cho - sen ones__ will flourish in the light of Christ the Lord.
fear will not con - sume our be - ing nor the pale - ness of__ re - gret
Deeds of e - vil un - re - pent - ed will not pass the Sav - iour's test
Wit - ness - ing through - out__ the a - ges draw - ing o - thers to__ the Lord

NEDDY
8.7.8.7.D.

25

Lost, re - bel - lious souls in an - guish feel the might of Je - sus' sword.
touch the soul how - ev - er fleet-ing for we claim the Christ-paid debt.
but the right - eous are__ pre - sent-ed pure for their e - ter - nal rest.
we are named with - in__ the pag - es of the book of those re - stored.

May the Peace of God Go With You 127

*And the peace of God, which transcends all understanding, will guard
your hearts and your minds in Christ Jesus. Phil. 4:7*

Moderato ♩ = 75

May the peace of God go with you as you leave this place and His

coun - ten - ance of light shine for - ev - er on your face.

Copyright © 2010 Galley Music

JUNIOR AUSTIN
8.5.7.7.

128 Ye Servants of God

Ask the Lord of the harvest... to send out workers into His harvest field. Matt. 9:38

Moderato ♩ = 80

Charles C. Cooke

Ye ser - vants of God, go out___ to serve, Go

out___ in Je - sus' name___ to - day. Let His

peace and His love shine through ev - 'ry deed! Go

1. Optional ending

tend to His flock___ and faith - ful - ly feed.

MARJORIE LYNNE
9.8.11.10.

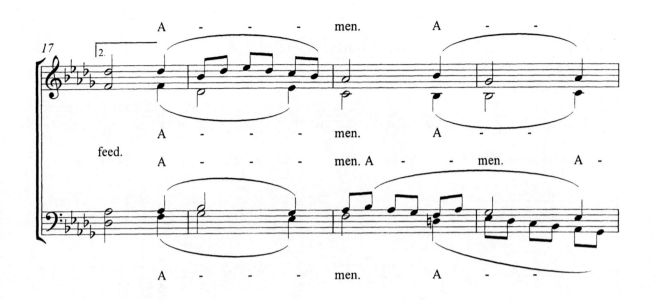

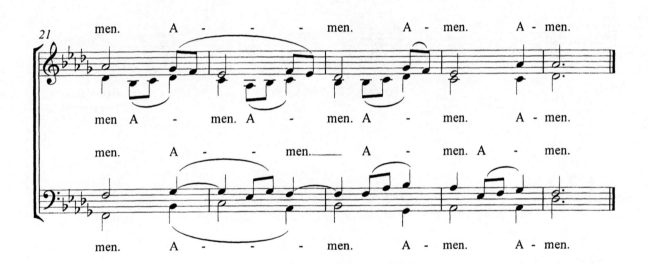

129   Be of Good Comfort

Text: 2 Cor. 13:11 (NKJV)

Charles C. Cooke

Moderato ♩ = 72

Be of good com-fort. Be of one mind. Live in peace. Live in peace; and the

God of peace and love will be with you. A - men. A men.

HOLETOWN
Irregular Meter

130   Grow in the Grace

Grow in the grace and knowledge of our Lord and Saviour Jesus Christ... 2 Peter 3:18

Andante ♩ = 66

Charles C. Cooke

Grow in the grace and know - ledge of our Lord and Sav-iour Je - sus Christ to

GROW IN THE GRACE
Irregular Meter

Him be glo - ry both now and for - ev - er.

The Grace of The Lord

131

May the grace of the Lord, Jesus Christ... be with you all. 2 Cor. 13:14

Charles C. Cooke

Andante ♩ = 66

May the grace of the Lord___ Je - sus Christ and the love___ of God and the

fel - low-ship of the Ho - ly___ Spir - it be___ with you all.

THE GRACE OF THE LORD
Irregular Meter

ALPHABETICAL INDEX OF HYMNS

INDEXES FOR THE HYMNS

ALPHABETICAL INDEX OF SONGS in the TAIZÉ STYLE

METRICAL INDEX OF TUNES

INDEXES FOR THE HYMNS

INDEX OF SCRIPTURE APPEARING
WITH HYMN TITLES

Genesis		84:1	112	**Matthew**	
1:1	4	86:6	35	4:4	65
Exodus		99:8	11	6:1	105
4:2	92	106:47	83	6:14	95
Deuteronomy		119:64	7	6:19	28
33:3, 27	119	119:165	117	9:38	128
2 Chronicles		120:1	51	11:28	97, 98
7:14	40	121:5	45	20:31	88
20:21	100	121:5,7	27	21:9	72
Nehemiah		122:7	41	24:35	3
8:10	19	126:2	24	25:40	110
13:31	90	127:3	63	26:26	70
Job		136:7-9	6	26:36	69
42:5	108	145:5	8	27:62	73
Psalms		146:6	10	**Mark**	
4:8	14	149:1	2	10:9	99
8:2	62	**Proverbs**		13:32	123
10:14	61	2:6	103	**Luke**	
16:11	9	3:7	91	1:30,31	57
19:1	5	15:13	18	2:7	58
23:5	87	16:3	15	2:8	60
25:5	38	**Ecclesiastes**		4:14,15	66
25:8	31	1:8	13	9:51	67
27:14	50	**Isaiah**		18:16	64
31:16,19	29	9:6	42	22:62	94
32:7	113	35:8	54	**John**	
34:4	47	43:19	43	3:16	75, 77
34:8	23	46:4	118	4:35	109
42:1	46	56:7	36	6:35	85
43:1	89	**Lamentations**		16:16	68
46:10	39	5:21	37	17:4	76
47:2	1	**Joel**		19:34	86
51:10	12	3:2	108	21:3	121
65:1-2	21	**Jonah**		**Acts**	
68:3	22	2:8	29	4:12	84
71:1	16	**Malachi**		16:31	32
73:26	49	3:10	101		

INDEXES FOR THE HYMNS

INDEX OF KEYS

MAJOR KEYS

Key of A
O Faithful, Bring Your Praises — 20

Key of Ab
Come In Silence Before The Lord — 40
From the Realms of Kingship Glory — 59
Go and Be Reconciled — 95
God's Rest for Which We Strive — 125
Hear, O Hear My Prayer — 35
His Comfort is Given to Those Who Grieve — 115
His Eyes Hath Never Left My Frame — 45
In His Care — 114
In The Inn of Bethlehem — 58
O Guide Me — 38
Still Our Hope Is In The Lord — 48
The Earth Is Filled With Your Love — 7

Key of Bb
Are You Ready? — 106
Do Not Be Weary — 96
How Happy Are The Faithful! — 18
Jesus Sealed the Master Plan — 69
Keep Thy Servant Close Forever — 27
Let Those Who Serve Be Counted — 104
Night Recedes Forevermore — 124
O Blessed Jesus, Prince of Peace — 42
O The Righteous Are Glad — 22
We All Need Christian Fellowship — 93
What Fleeting Praise We Often Seek! — 105

Key of C
A Vessel Prepared — 33
Be of Good Comfort — 129
Come, Gracious Spirit, Fill My Soul — 81
Fill Us, Fill Us With Your Grace — 79
From Nothing You Created Heaven and Earth — 4
Gifted From the God of Grace — 63
God Is So Good — 31

Grow in Grace — 130
Life Beyond the Golden Sunset — 122
Lord, God in You I Trust — 16
Lord, The Fields Are White for Harvest — 109
Never Go Hungry — 94
Not Ours to Know — 123
Our Tongues With Joyful Shouting — 24
Praise Awaits You O God in Zion — 21
Remain In Me — 68
Saviour, When I Am Uncertain — 89
Seek The Lord and He Will Hear Us — 47
Show Us the Better Way, O Lord — 111
Strength in Waiting Is Our Goal — 50
The Dusty Roads He Walked — 66
The Eternal God Is Your Refuge — 119
The Fruit of Self-Control — 53
The Joy of the Lord — 19
The Sunrise Shows Your Faithfulness — 10
The Way of Holiness — 54
Thy Healing Power Is Always Near — 87

Key of D
Bring Your Gifts to God — 101
By Night God's Glory Was Revealed — 60
God Is the Strength of My Long Aching Heart — 49
Great Peace Have Those Who Love Your Law — 117
I Have Heard of You — 107
Lord, I Desire to Worship You — 11
More of Jesus I Would Want — 102
O Christ, The First and Last — 77
O, That We Might Humble Be — 34
On The Day That Has No Name — 73
Sing Praises to the Lord! — 2
Those Who Cling to Worthless Idols — 29
Trusting, Trusting Little Children — 62
When Two Are Joined in Perfect Love — 99
Lord, Hear The Cry of Those Who Dwell — 108

INDEXES FOR THE HYMNS

INDEXES FOR THE HYMNS

CPSIA information can be obtained at www.ICGtesting.com
Printed in the USA
LVOW09s1123090813

347012LV00001B/1/P